YORK NOTES

General Editors: Professor A.N. Jeffares (*University of Stirling*) & Professor Suheil Bushrui (*American University of Beirut*)

Ben Jonson

THE ALCHEMIST

Notes by Andrew Gurr

MA (AUCKLAND) PH D (CAMBRIDGE)
Professor of English, University of Reading

LONGMAN
YORK PRESS

YORK PRESS
Immeuble Esseily, Place Riad Solh, Beirut.

ADDISON WESLEY LONGMAN LIMITED
Edinburgh Gate, Harlow,
Essex CM20 2JE, England
Associated companies, branches and representatives
throughout the world

First published 1981
Eleventh impression 1998

ISBN 0-582-03361-6

Printed in Singapore through Addison Wesley Longman China Limited

Contents

Part 1

Introduction

Jonson's life

Ben Jonson was born in London in the summer of 1572. His father, who was probably a churchman, died before he was born. His mother was soon married again, to a man who was a master bricklayer in Westminster, close to the City of London. They were not wealthy, and although Jonson was educated at Westminster School, one of the best schools in London, he did not go on to further study at university. His teacher at Westminster was William Camden, one of the best scholars of the day, and going to university would have helped him in social status more than in learning. Jonson had in any case an aggressive streak which made him, despite his relatively short career as a student, one of the foremost scholars of his time. He became expert in Greek as well as Roman classical texts. Perhaps it was his pride in his self-made scholarship which made him comment patronisingly on his old friend Shakespeare that he had 'small Latin and less Greek'. Neither playwright needed more than a grammar-school education for their great achievements, but Jonson's drive and aggression made him discontented with anything less than first place in public esteem. His pride in his own achievements perhaps led him to value learning beyond its natural worth.

His upbringing also made him insecure socially. He probably worked as an apprentice for his stepfather when he left school, eventually becoming a qualified bricklayer. He evidently did not like the work because he soon enlisted as a soldier and fought in the Netherlands, where the Dutch were fighting to free themselves from the control of Catholic Spain. In later years his enemies mocked him for having started life as a bricklayer. One even wrote:

> But to advise thee, Ben, in this strict age,
> A brickhill's fitter for thee than a stage.
> Thou better knows a groundsel [foundation wall] how to lay
> Than lay the plot or groundwork of a play.

Thin-skinned and truculent, Jonson was easily vulnerable to this kind of sneer.

His achievements as a poet and playwright from the age of twenty-six, at a time when competition for favour and money was brutal, also set him up high as a target for his rivals. He attracted trouble like a magnet. In 1597 when he was beginning his stage career as an actor he fought a duel with another actor and killed him. He fought a duel of another kind with Inigo Jones, who did the staging for the court masques which Jonson wrote, over a period of thirty years. In life and art alike he was forceful and assertive.

He married in 1596, and had several children. In 1619, after more than twenty-five years of marriage, he described his wife to a friend as 'a shrew, but honest'. She had by then been given a lot to put up with. Her husband had been put in prison three times, once under threat of death, had suffered financial troubles, had changed his religion, had taken up with other women, and had proved himself incapable of staying at home for any length of time. In the mid-1590s, when he was making his way as an actor and hack writer for the acting companies, he was obliged to travel with the players. Once that was no longer necessary he still travelled regularly for pleasure. He seems to have lived apart from his wife for some lengthy periods.

He must have been quite successful in the last of the careers he tried before he was able to write full time, acting. While a travelling player he probably took the role of Hieronymo, the lead part in Thomas Kyd's (1557?-1595?) *Spanish Tragedy* (1587) one of the most famous plays of the day. In 1597 he was taken on by Philip Henslowe, the most successful London impressario and theatre-owner. His period of working for Henslowe, however, did not last long. In the same year he was put in prison for writing a satirical play, and in the following year he killed Gabriel Spencer, an actor who had been imprisoned with him. For this he lost all his goods and was branded on the thumb. While in prison, too, he became a Catholic, the faith he had fought against in the Netherlands, and which was regarded with deep suspicion and hostility by the authorities. In its time and place this conversion seems almost a calculated act of defiance. He returned to the Church of England in about 1610.

By the time of his fight with Henslowe's actor, Jonson had changed his employer. His first successful stage hit, *Every Man in his Humour*, had just been performed by Shakespeare's company. From this time, September 1598, onwards he was famous, and a career as a writer was assured. A company of boy actors took on another of his plays, *The Case is Altered*, Shakespeare's company staged the sequel to *Every Man In*, and he even returned to write for Henslowe, in collaboration with Thomas Dekker. Possibly because his nature made it easier for him to work with children than with adult employers, his plays written between 1600 and 1604 *(Cynthia's Revels, Poetaster* and *Epicene)* were all written for a boy company. His involvement as leading satirist on one side in the so-called War of the Theatres, in which *Poetaster*

(1601) and *Cynthia's Revels* (1601) were salvoes, is evidence both of his touchiness and of his fame. The War was good publicity for the theatres, but the satirical portraits of Jonson in the salvoes by John Marston and others contain more venom than was called for by an advertising campaign.

The caricatures of him were certainly wounding enough to make him leave society for a while after 1602. This was probably the time of his long absence from his wife. He stayed with one wealthy patron after another while he wrote both comedies and tragedies. One comedy, *Eastward Ho!* (1605), got him into prison once more with one of his co-authors, because of its satire against the new king's Scottish followers. He was also in trouble over his tragedy *Sejanus* (1603). Despite the government's displeasure, though, he was from this time on employed in writing royal entertainments. From 1605 he was the chief provider of court masques. He became the 'King's Poet', the first real Poet Laureate of England.

In 1605 he gave Shakespeare's company *Volpone*, but then left them again until he returned with *The Alchemist* in 1610. It is possible that they approached him for a play on this later occasion. The boy companies had fallen into disrepute and financial difficulties for the sharpness of their satires, and Shakespeare's company had taken over their best playhouse, the Blackfriars, in 1609. As we know from the reference in I.i.17 and elsewhere, *The Alchemist* was written for this theatre. Possibly Jonson was invited to contribute a play because of his familiarity with the playhouse and its audience's familiarity with his plays. Equally it may be that Shakespeare was on the point of retiring to Stratford and the company hoped that Jonson would take his place as resident playwright.

If this was the case, they were disappointed. Jonson was always a travelling man and never stayed long with one employer. Moreover he now had no reason to commit himself to any employment. Although the years following *The Alchemist* did not by any means mark the end of controversy in his life, they did mark the time when his fame as a writer became entirely secure. The prosperity which this security gave him also brought him freedom from the hack-writing and collaborative writing which he had been obliged to undertake in his earlier years.

Security also freed him to develop the scholarly basis of his writing. This is most evident in his poetry, which flourished at its best in these years, although it also appears in the plays. *The Alchemist's* language is partly based on a careful study of alchemical texts and the mysteries which the elaborate jargon of alchemy concealed. Scrupulously marshalled learning also lies behind his Roman tragedy *Catiline*, written in the year following *The Alchemist*, and in the classical mythology from which he derived the materials for his masques. But in none of these works did his learning, paraded in full view though it was, overcome his central idea, the mission to educate.

Nor did it make him a pedant in society. In his company wit sparkled. We have ample tributes to the fun young men of wit found with him, in the verse letters which Francis Beaumont and Thomas Coryat wrote. Beaumont warmly records the delights of meeting at the Mermaid tavern:

> Methinks the little wit I had is lost
> Since I saw you, for wit is like a rest
> Held up at tennis, which men do the best
> With the best gamesters; what things have we seen
> Done at the Mermaid! heard words that have been
> So nimble and so full of subtle flame
> As if that every one from whence they came
> Had meant to put his whole soul in a jest
> And had resolved to live a fool the rest
> Of his dull life.*

Some discreet references in his poems and elsewhere suggest that ladies also found his company a pleasure.

His popularity in the tavern and in great houses was not matched, however, by the popularity of his plays on stage at this time. He continued to be highly sensitive to public opinion. After the success of *The Alchemist* his next play *Catiline* was condemned by everyone when it was staged in 1611. It was three years before he put another play on stage, and then it was with materials as far removed from the solemnly learned Roman rhetoric of *Catiline* as possible: the comic celebration of London life in *Bartholomew Fair* (1614). One more comedy followed, but otherwise for ten years he wrote only poems, masques and learned essays in history. His collected plays, which he called his *Works*, appeared in folio, the most grandiose form of publication, in 1616. Considering how ready he was to see playwriting as a hackwork that was perhaps a little surprising. Some of his contemporaries however saw it as downright arrogance, and that view has some truth in it. Jonson had a theory of comedy, and knew that he had written the best comedies in English to support his theory. It was right to advertise their stature. He was to be measured against the classical Roman writers, and would not be found wanting. His famous poem, the 'Execration upon Vulcan', written in 1623 after a fire had destroyed his papers, shows how much he felt his status came from his learning and put him equal in stature to the Latin writers.

The Works of Francis Beaumont and John Fletcher, edited by A. Glover and A. R. Waller, 10 vols, Cambridge University Press, Cambridge 1905-12, X, 200.

It was in this period, in 1618, that Jonson journeyed to Scotland. There he stayed with the poet Drummond of Hawthornden, a quiet soul who recorded his impressions of Jonson with memorable honesty. Jonson told Drummond that he was 'too good and simple, and that often a man's modesty made a fool of his wit'. Drummond clearly registered Jonson's own immodesty.

> He is a great lover and praiser of himself, a contemner and scorner of others, given rather to lose a friend than a jest, jealous of every word and action of those about him (especially after a drink, which is one of the elements in which he liveth), a dissembler of ill parts which reign in him, a bragger of some good that he wanteth, thinketh nothing well but what either he himself or some of his friends and countrymen hath said or done. He is passionately kind and angry, careless either to gain or keep, vindictive, but if he be well answered, at himself . . . Interpreteth best sayings and deeds often to the worst, oppressed with fantasy, which hath ever mastered his reason, a general disease in many poets.

Jonson was in Scotland as a tourist, and evidently enjoyed telling travellers' tales far from home. He gave his host a quantity of gossip and opinion which would hardly have been so colourful if he had been closer to London and if his host had known his subjects at first hand. So Drummond's view is jaundiced—the summary of a country poet overwhelmed by his urban guest and his wine bill. But Drummond's account of his lengthy conversations with Jonson, sage, gossip and drinker, rings true nevertheless. The universities honoured him, his friends loved him, and some of his hosts found him too boisterous for their comfort.

The last twenty years of Jonson's life, till his death in 1637, are generally seen as a long period in which he declined as a playwright. Oxford gave him an honorary degree in 1619, and he subsequently lectured on rhetoric at Gresham College in London. Between 1616 and 1626 he wrote nothing for the stage. When he did return to playwriting, for money, he found polemic, attacks on what he saw as social evils, easier than art. A man who so depended on praise to make him feel secure and whose aggressiveness made so many enemies, he inevitably found it hard not to over-react to public opinion. Surrounded by loyal followers, who were called in a biblical joke 'the Tribe of Ben', after one of the twelve tribes of Israel, and attacked by the men his principles led him to criticise, he must have found it difficult to judge his own writing dispassionately. Very little of his work through this period is not an attack or a defence of some sort, with varying degrees of justification and varying success. His comedy *A Staple of News* (1626) brilliantly attacked the vices of the new art of journalism, but less justifiable targets or less well-calculated assaults often vitiated his later work.

Partly paralysed by a stroke in 1628, he began to suffer obscurity and poverty for the second time. For the first five years of Charles I's reign, from 1625, the court commissioned nothing from him. He wrote a few plays for money, without the cutting edge of his earlier satires. *The Magnetic Lady*, staged in 1632, is a powerful exception to this pattern, but even this brought more hostility from Jonson's enemies than support from his friends. The court came to his aid occasionally, but a revival of the old feud with Inigo Jones over staging his masques limited his success. The Tribe of Ben, who still came regularly to his bedside in Westminster, revered him for his poetry rather than his plays. He was sixty-five when he died, having outlived all his contemporaries, the legitimate father of a whole generation of poets.

The theatre in Jonson's time

Jonson's dealings with his chief employers, the acting companies, were variable and often stormy. The acting companies had grown in status and wealth up to the end of the sixteenth century in London till they were more powerful than they had ever been. They were a product, like Jonson himself, of the new literacy which followed the growth of printed books and the development of an education system to use them. The first proper theatre was built in London in 1576. Twenty years later, when Jonson was turning from acting to writing plays for the actors, the leading companies had a great reputation, real wealth, and a huge appetite for new plays.

An acting company was usually ten or twelve men who shared the costs and the profits amongst themselves, and who trained apprentices (boys who played the female roles) and hired men on a casual basis for the lesser parts. Supporting most of the acting groups there was a financier, the theatre owner, who would hire out properties and even play-texts to the company. Only Shakespeare's company, for which *The Alchemist* was written, was a truly co-operative venture in which the actors were the shareholders and financiers. Besides the two or three resident adult companies, acting groups consisting entirely of boys flourished between 1600 and 1608, and in these the financier was also the company manager. All the companies performed in the afternoons on every day of the week except Sundays. Each day the play would be different. Even the most popular plays were rarely put on more than once in every three or four weeks. Consequently the actors needed prodigious memories and had little time for subtlety either in acting or staging. A 'book-keeper' sat behind the stage with a list of cues and the properties needed for each scene. But the stage area was large and the audiences noisy, so that once an actor was out on the stage the book-keeper could do little to prompt him if he forgot his part. Actors dared not hesitate anyway. Nonstop speech and action were necessary to dominate the restless audience, many of whom would be standing throughout the performance.

The rise of the acting companies, like the rise of the playwrights such as Shakespeare and Jonson from a relatively low social status, is a mark of the social mobility of the time. The audiences who came to the plays came similarly from all social levels. In the first theatres everyone gathered together, as many as three thousand at a time. One penny bought standing room near the stage. More pennies bought a seat in the galleries, and sixpence bought a box alongside the stage. In 1600 when the boy companies started performing commercially in London they used a smaller kind of theatre with seating for only six hundred and a minimum price of sixpence. The old theatres were round amphitheatres open to the sky. The new theatres were enclosed halls. Gradually this new kind of indoor theatre became the favourite type, and established the shape most theatres still have today. The Blackfriars, where *The Alchemist* was first performed, was of this second type.

Jonson's involvement in the acting world reflects these features in various ways. The adult acting companies who were his main employers frequently annoyed him by the casualness with which they handled his texts. They were his employers, and could do as they pleased with what he sold them. Most companies had resident playwrights. Shakespeare not only acted for his company but sold them two plays a year for nearly twenty years. Dekker wrote for the financier Henslowe as many as four or five plays a year, besides collaborating with other writers. This brought him perhaps £20 in a good year, rather less than an actor could expect. Jonson seems to have started writing for Henslowe, switched to Shakespeare's company for two or three years, and left them for the boy companies as soon as they got going. The boys were more biddable than the adult actors. Besides its share in the War of the Theatres, *Cynthia's Revels,* which Jonson wrote in 1601, is a manual on how boys should act. He could never have ordered the adults around in the same way.

After his early stint of writing for the boy companies Jonson had a good deal of financial security. While he lodged with his wealthy patrons he sent his plays to different companies at wide intervals of time. *Volpone* was performed by Shakespeare's company in 1605. *Epicene* was done by a boy company in 1609, *The Alchemist* for Shakespeare's company in late 1610, when there were no boy companies acting in London. He stayed with the same company for

Catiline in 1611, but went to another adult company with *Bartholomew Fair* in 1614. In this period, and especially in the later years of King James's reign, he wrote more masques for the court than plays for the town. For all his bravado in calling them his *Works*, there was always a consciously financial motive behind his writing of plays, and perhaps an awareness that it was a less respectable occupation than writing poetry, masques and lectures on grammar and art.

Nonetheless he put heart and soul into his plays, and was shattered by the hostile reception of his two tragedies. His comedies were a moral duty, the ridiculing of folly, corrective and therefore in a sense negative. His tragedies were positive assertions of intellectual and moral values. As positive declarations Jonson valued them highly, but they were also more vulnerable to criticism than the comedies. His attitude to popular acclaim was always mixed, though he records gratefully the high praise given to *Volpone* when it was performed at the universities. In fact his comedies were his greatest achievement and his own variable opinion can never alter that.

Jonson's theory of comedy

Jonson evolved a theory of comedy which was moral and educative. No clear-cut idea of comedy survived from classical times of the sort Aristotle (384-322BC), the famous Greek philosopher-critic, provided for tragedy in his *Poetics*. Cicero, Horace and Terence, the chief Latin writers on comic theory, all had their formulas, but there was no one clear pattern. The Renaissance extended the scope of classical ideas by adding romance to the subject-matter. Shakespeare's comedies owe much less of a debt to classical comedy than to the romantic tales of the Middle Ages and the Renaissance. So Jonson was to a large extent free to develop his own theory of what comedy in the theatre could and should do.

Cicero had maintained that comedy holds a mirror up to human life. Horace had asserted more specifically that it should be a criticism of human behaviour. Vice and folly were its targets, mockery and ridicule its weapons. The anti-social should be laughed to shame or at least humiliated. The old English tradition of morality plays and interludes (short plays teaching Christian morals, popular in the fifteenth and sixteenth centuries) had a similar aim, in the particular shape of demonstrating Christian morality. Jonson saw the possibility that the theatre could not just mirror human manners but could criticise bad manners, and constructed his own theory accordingly. In his early plays he added two elements to the traditional patterns. First he put on stage characters from the life of contemporary London, especially the low life of thieves and cheats, with an accuracy never before seen on stage. Secondly he made into a doctrine the idea that normality in human conduct, the golden mean, was a positive ideal and that comedy could affirm the ideal through ridicule of human eccentricity. Hence his theory of humours and his gulling comedy.

The first innovation, realistic portrayal of London life, was an integral part of his theory, though sometimes it got him into trouble. Time and time again he declared that he was attacking vices and follies, not the people in real life who displayed them. 'My books have still been taught/To spare the persons and to speak the vice' he wrote in *Poetaster*, a claim he repeated in the prologues to *Epicene, The Alchemist, Bartholomew Fair* and other plays. Of course, if everyone is potentially normal, if folly and vice are aberrations, such a distinction can be made. But the Scotsman who complained to King James and got Jonson put into prison for the caricatures of the Scots in *Eastward Ho!* did not think so. Certainly the confidence tricks played in *The Alchemist* were based on real events and real people. For Jonson the success of his comedies depended on his audiences recognising what they saw on stage as an image of reality. He was aiming not at particular fools, but at the audiences who would see themselves depicted as fools. It was his audiences whom he hoped to educate in the moral art of recognising the norms of human behaviour.

Jonson's second development in comedy, the gulling principle, appears in his first plays as part of the theory of humours. This was the theory that human physiology incorporates four main elements or qualities, the liquids phlegm, blood, yellow bile or choler, and black bile or melancholy. In balance with each other these four liquids or 'humours' produced a balanced or normal personality. Out of balance a character would become 'humorous': phlegmatic, sanguine, choleric or melancholic according to which humour was in excess. The phlegmatic or cold and dry humour produced dull and dreary characters; sanguine or hot and moist characters were lecherous (Dol Common is called sanguine at II.iv.11); choleric or hot and dry characters were irritable; while the melancholic or cold and moist humour was depressive, like Abel Drugger (III.iv.107). Medical treatment for unbalanced humours included bloodletting for the sanguine, that is removing some of the excess blood. The cold were given warmth, the dry were prescribed drink and so on. Jonson's comedy offered psychological treatment for the mental signs of imbalance in the same way that medicine was provided for the physical imbalance. His patients are 'gulled' or fooled, the audience recognises and laughs at their folly and is thus educated in the proper norm of human conduct.

The idea of treating follies and vices as if they were medical ailments is important because to some extent it replaced the traditional idea that vices should be punished. Jonson's comedy in the 'humours' plays and still more in the later masterpieces was more concerned with reform in the audience than with punishment of the stage characters. When he displays vice in a comedy, as in *Volpone,* the final punishment is necessary more for reasons of art than of justice. When his chief targets are folly rather than vice, as in *The Alchemist,* the fools are laughed out of their folly and the villains are simply returned to the position they had occupied at the outset of the play. Jonson's moral impulse was powerful, but it was controlled by a theory of comedy as a primarily educative art which gave his plays a level of sophistication far beyond the moral interludes of the English comic tradition he inherited, which always insisted on ending with the punishment of the bad. At the end of *The Alchemist* Lovewit gets away with a load of undeserved wealth because in Jonson's comic art the audience's response demands a conclusion more complex than simple justice.

A note on the text

The Alchemist was first published in 1612, and again in a more carefully prepared version in the collected *Works* in 1616. This second edition was checked by Jonson himself and has been used as the basis for all the major editions since. Unlike most editions of dramatic texts in Shakespeare's time it supplies in Jonson's own hand the necessary stage directions and the correct division into acts (when the stage is cleared of all the characters), and scenes (when a major character or group of characters makes an appearance).

The great modern edition of *The Alchemist* is in the complete edition of all Jonson's major works in eleven volumes, produced at Oxford by the Clarendon Press (now Oxford University Press) between 1925 and 1952. It was edited by C. H. Herford and Percy and Evelyn Simpson. *The Alchemist* appears in Volume 4. A general account of the play is in Volume 2, the printing of the text is discussed in Volume 9, and detailed notes on the text are supplied in Volume 10. All subsequent editions have based their text and most of their notes on the Herford and Simpson volumes. Good book-length editions include that in the Fountainwell Drama Texts series, Oliver and Boyd, Edinburgh, 1968, edited by S. Musgrove. This text retains Jonson's own spelling; it illustrates his use of apostrophes and other devices to indicate the pronunciation of elided phrases or words, and for the way it indicates puns which a modern spelling would conceal. Useful editions in modern spelling include the New Mermaid Edition, Benn, London, 1966, edited by Douglas Brown.

Part 2

Summaries

of THE ALCHEMIST

A general summary

The story of *The Alchemist* is the performance of an elaborate confidence trick. A trickster (or 'cozener) and his woman have met a servant, a butler who is looking after his master's town house while his master is hiding in the country from the current epidemic of bubonic plague. The two cozeners agree with the servant to use the house as their base for tricking various fools out of their wealth. To do this the male cozener pretends to be an alchemist, a magician of pseudo-science, who will give his clients magic powers in return for cash. The butler poses as his assistant and marshals the victims, whom he meets in the taverns and eating houses of London, and whom he invites to visit the alchemist at his house.

All the characters have names indicating their roles. The alchemist Subtle's name indicates his profession of cozener. Latin *subtilis* means shrewd, like the modern subtle, but also plain in speech. It derives from *sub-tela,* a web, and implies that Subtle is a man who catches his victims in a web of words, like a spider. In appearance on stage he is dark-complexioned. Twice he is called a collier, once 'black boy', and his colour is said to be 'of the Roman [or gypsy] wash'. Colliers and magicians were both thought to be related to the anti-Christian powers of darkness. Subtle is a devilish spider. The butler Face is a dissembler too, a man of many faces. Dol Common, the third cozener, is a creature the others use like a toy (a doll), and who is a piece of shared property (Common, their commonwealth, or *res publica).* As a prostitute she is common property to anyone who will pay for her services. The victims of these three cozeners are an assortment of typical London characters of the time, ranging in social status from a shopkeeper (Drugger) to a wealthy knight (Mammon). Abel Drugger sells cosmetics and drugs, including tobacco. Dapper is a law student who has hopes of making himself a dashing young man about town by gambling and dressing expensively. The Puritans, many of whom lived in the Blackfriars precinct where the theatre for which the play was written was situated, both have the standard kind of names which Puritans used to give themselves at this time. Tribulation exemplifies the fashion for making one's name a reminder of the nature of piety. Ananias, who in the Bible (Acts 5) was a liar, was also a Puritan name, because the Puritans considered that all men are sinners and therefore any name at all from the Bible is acceptable.

Sir Epicure Mammon gets his first name from the school of Greek philosophers, the Epicureans, who were regarded as sensualists denying any divinity but that of their own senses. His second name is that of the devil who tempts men into the sin of avarice. Pertinax Surly, another trickster, who makes his living by cheating at card games, is also described in both of his names. *Pertinax* is Latin, meaning obstinate. Surly implies a sullen or phlegmatic 'humour', slow and suspicious in temperament. Dame Pliant has a name which similarly describes her docile character. Kestrel, or Kastril as Jonson spelled it, the 'angry boy', is a kestrel, one of the smallest kinds of hawk. The name fits his ambition to become a good picker of quarrels, a small bird of prey. In reality he is that other kind of bird the gull, a fool, as much as any of the other victims.

Finally the master of the house, Lovewit, who returns in Act V to find his house has been visited with a different kind of plague, is a lover of fertile wit. He says so at his first appearance on stage at V.i.16. Wit in this sense is the opposite of the foolishness which all the gulls display. Face manages to get Lovewit's support by the unlikely trick of telling him the truth, and as a result Lovewit emerges at the end of the play as the only character who gets away with the loot.

The play works by the traditional device of most comedy, inversion. Normality is turned upside down to show its ridiculous side and to underline the nature of true reality. The master-servant relationship between Lovewit and Face as his butler, for instance, is inverted. Subtle turns from his normal role of cozener at the bottom of the social ladder to being a king in the little republic of gulling. The house in which he is a furtive tenant becomes his kingdom. Mammon the wealthy knight and the Puritan brethren reverse the proper roles of nobles and priests in society out of greed for their personal gain. All the main social values are inverted in the process.

The metaphor which embodies this inversion in the play is that of alchemy. Alchemy claimed to transform or transmute one quality to a higher quality. Its advocates were either deluded or deceitful in making the claim. Anyone believing in such transformations is a fool, and likely to be gulled. Anyone believing it and pretending he does believe is a cozener. Either way truth is lost sight of in the inversion of reality. On stage the cozeners rapidly change their costumes to fit the delusions of their different clients. When they do so the audience gets a visual reminder of how truth is being obscured in the pursuit of personal gain. It is obscured because greed and self-interest make some men gullible and others willing to cozen and cheat them. An inverted society such as the republic of the would-be alchemists in the play is the product of inverted social values which put the self before the social good. The play invites its audience to recognise the social values which the delusion shown by the metaphor of alchemy is inverting.

The language of the play presents these inversions through a series of recurrent metaphors. The house is a country within a country. Subtle is its king, Face its general, and the whole house is a citadel or military camp fortified against the rest of the world. Mammon calls the house a *novum orbis*, the Latin for a new world, by analogy with the Americas which were then new enough to have no settled societies and therefore no laws of a kind that Europeans could recognise, and which were being exploited for gold. In another image the cozeners are dogs and the gulls are different kinds of birds ('unclean birds' the Puritans claim) who are being eaten by the beasts of prey. Christianity is likewise inverted, and Mammon appears as a reversal of everything that Christian values uphold. The Puritans too are a transformed variety of Christian. They hypocritically justify their own greed on the grounds that their separate society of 'brethren' possesses a religious truth superior to that of the society in which they live. Thus they are justified, they think, in exploiting that society.

The overriding metaphor of alchemy embraces all of these images. Alchemy was made such a deliberately obscure art that it could embody religious, political, military, medical, commercial and even sexual images. Even the plot itself can be seen as an alchemical image. It comes to the boil as more and more ingredients (the play's characters) are thrown in until it explodes like Subtle's own potion. What follows the explosion is a matter of picking up such pieces as can be rescued from the mess. In the process the quickest-witted gets away with everything.

Detailed summaries

Prefaces

The printed text of the play begins with a dedication to Lady Wroth, a niece of Sir Philip Sidney, the poet (1554-1586), and an Epistle to the Reader. Both of these contain indications of Jonson's ideas and intentions in writing the play which will be looked into later. Thirdly it has an *Argument,* a poem which is an acrostic in which the first letter of each line spells out the play's title, which was also provided only for the printed text of the play.

The Prologue, which opens the play as it was staged in 1610, contains most of the main points made in the three prefaces supplied for the printed text. It is addressed directly to the theatre audience, the 'judging spectators'. It describes the subject, the 'manners, now called humours' of contemporary London. There is a hint of moral reproof in this reference to the current fashion in words. 'Manners' means moral conduct, the decorums of proper social behaviour. To call moral conduct a 'humour', meaning a whim or pecularity, implies that you are licensed to behave as your free will directs you. If you call your impulses 'humours' you are letting your passions govern your moral sense.

The function of the comic poet is to improve moral conduct, to make men behave better, and to do so without giving offence: 'this pen / Did never aim to grieve, but better men'. Also, Jonson declares, his moral medicine tastes sweet, so his audience will be grateful for it:

> He hopes to find no spirit so diseased
> But will with such fair correctives be pleased.

He openly hints however that the disease to be exposed in the play may be diagnosed among the members of the audience. This, of course, was exactly what his theory of comedy presumed. Fools can be made wise if they see their folly ridiculed in public. But Jonson moderates that ominous declaration at the end of the prologue with the promise that the 'natural follies' he will display will appear in such a way that only 'the doers' of such follies will recognise their own faults.

NOTES AND GLOSSARY:

faces of the time: people who falsify their appearance. Jonson is indirectly alluding to the play's central character

an understander: (a) a man who understands what he reads; (b) a spectator who stands around the stage at a performance of the play

cozened: cheated, tricked

the stone: the philosopher's stone, a device thought to give its owner power to change ordinary metals into gold. Alchemy was the science of making the philosopher's stone

spleen: bad temper, another 'humour'

Act I Scene i

The play itself begins startlingly. The theatre audience has had no previous warning that the three characters who storm in, the 'servant', the 'cheater' and his 'punk', as the Argument describes them for the reader, are partners. They erupt on stage shouting and swearing at each other. First Subtle and Face quarrel while Dol tries to make peace between them. Face, who as butler has the neighbours to think about, urges Subtle to speak more quietly. But Subtle provokes him till both are shouting foul names at each other and Dol has to break in and remind them of their 'venture tripartite'. Through the course of these first two hundred lines of the play, in shouts and whispers, the whole situation is made clear. They are a nation to themselves. The treaty or social contract which serves as their society's law is a commercial venture, an agreement called in V.v.131 an 'indenture tripartite'. This is the term used by the rebels in Shakespeare's *1 Henry IV* to signify their agreement over how they would share the territory once they had defeated the king. The quarrel between Subtle and Face which opens the play is a warning that this agreement, like that of Shakespeare's rebels, will not hold them together for long. Throughout the play Subtle and Face grumble about each other. And indeed once Lovewit returns to the house at the end of Act IV the treaty is readily broken. The opening scene illustrates the proverb about thieves falling out amongst themselves.

From Subtle's shouts and Face's hissing replies we learn what kind of thief each of them is. Face has always stolen from his master. Subtle's trick, unsuccessful enough to leave him nearly starving till he met Face, was to pretend to be a sorcerer of 'black arts'. He carries a phial in this scene, a test-tube full of his chemical potions which he waves around while he roars at Face. His speeches demonstrate his art of using language to deceive. Language is designed to communicate truths. Subtle inverts this design. The jargon or 'canting' (II.iii.42) language of alchemy was an early example of the familiar habit of baffling the hearer with science. Alchemical cant was designed to confuse the ignorant, as was the thieves' cant which also recurs throughout the play. William Gilbert (1540-1603), in a book of genuine science, *De Magnete,* 1600, wrote of how alchemists employed strange words and metaphors 'in order to veil things with a pedantic terminology and to make them dark and obscure'. Jonson like all his age valued language as God's gift to man, the unique quality which along with reason raised men above beasts. Cant, the immoral misuse of language to pervert man's reason, was a basic evil. Subtle's 'art' is an inversion of man's capacities.

It is a godless and fragile republic, the 'venture tripartite'. Dol compares Subtle and Face to barking dogs, beasts without the power of language or reason. Just as their language is inverted into cant so man's social impulse is inverted into a dog-eat-dog society. Later we shall see inversions extended, with science made into the tricks of alchemy and God replaced by Mammon. The republic has no laws to bind its members except gain. It puts no value on truth and is guided only by the advice 'Be rich!'

NOTES AND GLOSSARY:

wild sheep: an alchemical term for the dangerous liquid in the test-tube which Subtle holds. The alchemist was said to be a shepherd and his chemicals were his sheep, the same metaphor which appears in the Bible of Christ as shepherd and His congregation as a flock of sheep

livery-three-pound-thrum: a servant whose wage is £3 per year and who is dressed in odds and ends of cloth

suburb-captain: owner of a brothel. Surly identifies the house as a brothel at II.iii.226

sublimed . . . work: alchemical cant for the processes which would produce the stone

collier: a miner of coal. Being black-faced they were commonly linked with the devil

Gemaliel Ratsey: a Northamptonshire highwayman, widely known for the repulsive mask which he wore. He was executed in Bedford in 1605

republic: Dol is punning on her name, Dol Common. She is their 'commonwealth'

fermentation . . . cibation: more terms of alchemy

Sol and *Luna*: *(Latin)* sun and moon; in alchemical language gold and silver; also male and female

to see me ride: prostitutes were driven in a cart through the streets to be ridiculed

at the Dagger: in a tavern whose sign is a dagger

Act I Scene ii

We learn the exact nature of Subtle's cozening 'art' with the arrival of the first gull, Dapper. At the end of their quarrel, when they heard the first knock on the door at the end of I.i., each of the tricksters took up a role. Dol hides. She is to appear to Dapper later as the Queen of the Fairies. Subtle puts on the black gown of a doctor, a man of learning. Face goes to the door pretending to be a visitor on the point of leaving. He speaks of Dapper to the doctor as if he did not know Dapper was there to hear him. In this way the first gull is immediately established as a victim, one who knows far less than the audience what is going on.

Face's opening trick is to make Dapper more eager for the doctor's services by pretending reluctance. 'Read's matter' is the problem. Simon Read of Southwark in London had been brought to a court of law in 1608 under the statute which forbade the practice of necromancy, or magic. This reference to it reminds us that Dapper, a law student himself, is proposing to break the law for his own gain. At the same time it also reminds us just how local and specific were the materials Jonson used for his comedy. Dappers could be found as readily in the streets around Blackfriars as the 'sober, scurvy, precise neighbours', the Puritans whom Dol had voiced some fear of at I.i.164. Even the trick played on Dapper with the Queen of Faery was based on a trick played on a man called Thomas Rogers by Sir Anthony Ashley and his friends. That trick was the subject of a lawsuit while Jonson was writing his play, in 1609-10. A similar trick also came to the notice of the law in 1613.

Face's role here, as with some of the later gulls, is to act the part of 'Captain Face', a man about town who is a kind of courtier to Subtle the king. He is a go-between, presenting Dapper's petition to the reluctant monarch and pleading on his client's behalf as courtiers did to King James. The exchange between Face and Subtle in which Face pretends to argue Dapper's case provides him with an opportunity to abuse Subtle, in a neatly contrived continuation of the argument started in the previous scene. Such undertones do not of course prevent him from following his main objective of taking as much of Dapper's cash as he can get. The scene amply shows Dapper's greed and the gullibility which greed draws him into. Money is the only value anyone here acknowledges. When Dapper offers only an 'angel' in thanks to the doctor (a gold coin worth half a sovereign), Face reprimands him with 'What else is thanks? Will you be trivial?' (141). So he is set up to be properly gulled by his 'aunt' the Queen of Faery. He is sent off to clear the way for the next gull, and told to return at 1 p.m. ready to meet his 'aunt' and his 'fortune'

NOTES AND GLOSSARY:

the statute:	the law against necromancy which Face mentions at I.i.112
chouse:	Turkish *chaush,* a herald. A Turk who gave himself that title swindled London merchants in 1607. It became a fashionable word for a cheat. Face mocks Dapper's use of fashionable slang by repeating his word to Subtle
a familiar	a spirit which will spy for him. Dapper wants a small one in the shape of an insect to tell him what to gamble on

dead Holland, living Isaac: Dutch alchemists, father and son

Act I Scene iii

In this scene the next gull, Drugger, shows how gullibility corresponds to social status. For Dapper Subtle posed as a learned doctor and necromancer. For Mammon, the chief gull, he will be the saintly alchemist. But for the humble shopkeeper Abel Drugger Subtle is just an astrologer who will cast his horoscope and so provide guidance for his business. The humbler the gull, the more credulous he is. Drugger is presented by Face to Subtle as an honest seller of tobacco, though Face describes the tricks of his trade in a way which suggests that he is familiar with the ways of being dishonest. He does not offer rich pickings—as Face warns Subtle, he is "no goldsmith". Goldsmiths, apart from dealing in the most precious commodity of all, also ran the beginnings of a banking system. Subtle notes Face's warning and develops the double-talk as he cozens Drugger with his cant. He notes that Drugger was born under Libra (line 56), and asserts that the 'lord of his horoscope' is Mercury, the god of commerce. In fact it was Venus, the goddess of love. In a similar way Subtle tempts Drugger with the hope of finding the philosopher's stone by means of the drugs and chemicals he sells. This prepares us for the more elaborate bait Subtle is going to offer to the chief gulls, Mammon and the Puritans.

NOTES AND GLOSSARY:

free of the Grocers: a member of the Guild of Shopkeepers
called to the scarlet: be appointed sheriff of London
my intelligence:　Face's information about possible gulls

Act I Scene iv

At the end of the first act we have a brief exchange between the three 'venturers' which reminds us of their underlying enmity. Face reminds Subtle of all his hard work in finding gulls, and how much it costs him, a claim Subtle loftily disregards. Dol then enters with news of her catch of gulls, making it clear that Face is not the only catcher. The quarrel is cut off by Dol's announcement that Sir Epicure Mammon, the highest-ranking of all the gulls, is outside the house. The Act ends with an account of Mammon's dream of grandeur—'If his dream last, he'll turn the age to gold', that is, he will bring back the glories of the golden age by means of the philosopher's stone and all the gold which it will bring him. Ambition for glory and greed for gold are summed up in that one phrase.

NOTES AND GLOSSARY:

Through the trunk: through a tube, to make the voice sound disembodied

Act II Scene i

Making the philosopher's stone was the aim of every alchemist. Solomon was said to have achieved it, and alchemists of the Renaissance spent their lives trying to reproduce it. The theory was that all base metals should strive to turn into gold because gold is the perfection of all metals. With a philosopher of the supreme holiness necessary for perfection, and an unrivalled knowledge of chemistry, it was thought that a magic stone could be created which would be the instrument for converting base metals into their perfect form. In its holy perfection and its magic power it was thought that the stone was a confirmation of the wisdom and goodness of its owner. The goodness of course cancelled out any suggestion of greed. Mammon, who is a personification of greed, hopes that he will gain the absolute power of the stone through the holiness of his agent Subtle.

These grandiose dreams of the stone's power are voiced to the sceptical Surly in II.i. The house they are approaching, says Mammon, is *in novo orbe*, the new world—an ironical echo of the venture tripartite's *res publica*. Traditional society, its laws and its social values, are nothing to Mammon in his pursuit of the stone. His gospel is 'Be rich!' This is a parody of God's first words in the Book of Genesis in the Bible, *fiat lux*, let there be light. Mammon's ability to delude himself is clear even without his use of alchemical cant in lines 30-41. These lines measure the extent of the delusion. He follows alchemical practice in using the names of the planets for the various metals. Mercury (quicksilver, and also human wit), Venus (copper and love), and the Moon (silver and purity) are the metals Mammon will change into the sun (gold). Everything will be money. If we needed any confirmation of the wildness of his thinking this representation of the metals as planets changing into the sun provides it. The next lines offer yet more confirmation. Mercury was commonly used as a cure for a wide range of diseases, including venereal. To turn mercury into gold is metaphorically to make gold a medicine, just as Venus into gold makes love a matter of money. Mammon thinks he has the key to health, sexual potency, and eternal life with the stone. So he claims that the stone is also the elixir of life. *Aurum potabile* as he later names it in Latin, drinkable gold, was another fantasy of medieval science. Mammon confuses the two fantasies when he claims that the stone will give him the power of God to heal the sick, give youth to age and sexual potency to the impotent. All of Mammon's dreams are inversions of Christian belief, from the aim of 'Be rich!' (lines 7 and 24) to the culminating delusion that the stone will make him immortal. The real alchemists were more modest.

Surly's comments keep Mammon's balloon of excitement from floating clear off the earth, though Surly himself is no angel and his scepticism is not the same thing as truth. He is a professional cheat and cozener himself. He has seen nothing in his own life to make him believe Mammon's dream of easy money. He is simply down-to-earth. When Mammon speaks of Mars and Cupid, the gods of war and love, he speaks of the 'decayed Vestals' of London, the prostitutes. When Mammon speaks of the stone as a medicine to cure the plague he drily says that the players would be grateful. Since theatres were always shut when deaths by plague reached a certain number, his comment is appropriate. But it also serves to remind us of the local setting for Mammon's exotic dream. Later, when Mammon again speaks of the stone as having power to heal sickness Surly compares it to a gallstone.

This discussion all takes place in the street as Mammon and Surly approach the house. In Jonson's image the house is a fantasy world, the street reality. The gulls whom we see first in the street, Mammon and the Puritans, are typical of the regular inhabitants of the Blackfriars precinct. Moreover, Mammon as a gentleman of wealth and the Puritans as men of religion are supposed to be responsible citizens. The readiness with which they enter the house and plunge into delusion is a measure of how easy it is for the cozeners to invert the natural order of society. Later on, in Act V, the neighbours who appear in the street confirm the world's gullibility by the ease with which Face challenges their testimony even on their home ground.

NOTES AND GLOSSARY:

Solomon's Ophir: the wealth and wisdom of Solomon, the Old Testament patriarch, were said to have come from his possession of the philosopher's stone

his firedrake, His Lungs: Face's role with Mammon is that of the alchemist's helper, who works the bellows to heat the furnace

'Tis like your Irish wood . . .: Mammon's lists show what a learned fool he is. All his references have precedents in the sixteenth century. Jonson himself owned a copy of the manuscript on magic, allegedly written by Solomon, to which Mammon refers at line 82

Act II Scene ii

The scene when Mammon enters the house opens with a splendidly florid revelation of Mammon's unbounded appetite. His desires are a catalogue of everything that Christian society should condemn. He will have the whole world for himself. All women will be available to him and he will have sexual potency to match. His senses and his appetite will enjoy impossible luxury. All of it will be for him—Face must be castrated if he wants the benefits which will arise from his becoming Mammon's servant. Face gives discreet stimulus to the lavish verbiage of Mammon's dreams with his alchemical cant about the progress of the projection. Language is the chief instrument of self-delusion as well as cozening.

NOTES AND GLOSSARY:
projection: the final creation of the stone
my venture: Mammon sees the projection as a commercial adventure in the same terms as the cozeners see their partnership

---

Act II Scene iii

Here Subtle at last appears in his full glory, his most ambitious role, as the alchemist himself. For the chief gull, the grandest deception. Subtle pretends to be a holy man. He is the agent who will transmute dreams into reality by means of his purity and his learning. This pose, the opposite of truth both in piety and in language, is the central symbol of all the inversions and transmutations of the play. Out of his pretended piety Subtle reproves Mammon for his greed, fully aware, like the audience, that his own motive is pure greed. Surly compares his alchemical jargon to religious cant, the inverted language of hypocrisy.

Subtle displays his canting language in the discussions with Face about the 'work's' progress, and extracts money from Mammon (£10—line 93) to give it point. On receiving the money, Subtle declares to Face that 'two / Of our inferior works are at fixation, / A third is in ascension'. In front of Mammon he is using his cant to tell Face that Dapper and Drugger are ready for cozening ('at fixation') and that Mammon is well on the way. It remains to outface the sceptical challenge of Surly.

The bulk of Subtle's description of alchemy here, especially lines 131—76, was taken by Jonson nearly word for word from Martin Delrio's (1551—1608) *Disquisitiones Magicae* of 1599. He also took care to add the standard explanation for such complicated jargon (lines 199-201), that its purpose was to prevent fools from understanding the subject. There was a great deal of nonsense about alchemy available in Jonson's time. More than 113 texts on alchemy were printed between 1595 and 1615.

Surly is unconvinced by Subtle's parade of cant, and when he catches a glimpse of Dol he concludes the house must be a brothel. Dol is to become the means of sending Mammon away empty-handed without knowing he has been gulled. His lust for her will be Subtle's excuse for the failure of the projection. However when she appears on stage in this scene it is not at first clear that Mammon's sight of her is part of the plan. She appears when Mammon by chance uses the word 'common' which, of course, is her name (line 210). Subtle's shock and the oath he starts to swear might equally be genuine or part of his pious act. To Mammon he pretends that his holiness has been profaned by the sight of her, so he reprimands Face for allowing her to be seen. Face as usual is quick to exploit the situation and he tempts Mammon into believing that she is a lady ('a lord's sister', 221) who has been driven mad by reading 'Broughton's works'. Hugh Broughton was an eccentric Puritan and an astrologer who wrote a ludicrous commentary on the Bible. Dol quotes him word for word in IV.v.1-32 when her fit of pretended madness leads to the breaking of the alchemical projection.

The scene concludes with Mammon confirming how blind his greed is by telling lies to Surly, to convince him that Dol is not a whore. Mammon's self-deception leads him to deceive others. While he is doing this Face, as the alchemist's assistant, arranges for Surly to meet Face as Captain Face. He is setting up another bait for a gull. But Surly reveals in an aside that he sees through all the deception and will expose them. He will take over the gulling of Mammon himself (lines 310-11): 'You'll give your poor friend leave, though no philosopher, / To laugh: for you that are, 'tis thought, shall weep.' Impoverished Surly will laugh. Mammon for all his 'philosophy' will weep.

NOTES AND GLOSSARY:

Ulen Spiegel: Subtle gives his assistant the name of a German folk-hero. Many alchemists were German, including Paracelsus (1493-1541) and Faust (1488?-1541)

philosopher's wheel: the whole process of making the stone was thought of as cyclic. Hence it was symbolised as a wheel

a Bradamante: an Amazonian heroine in *Orlando Furioso* (1532), the Italian epic poem by Ludovico Ariosto (1474-1533)

Galen: the Roman physician (*c.*129-199) and father of orthodox herbal medicine. Paracelsus's chemical medicine was a challenge to his orthodoxy

a taste of her—wit—: Mammon's sensuality does not extend to women's minds

quicksilver/Or the hot sulphur: like the reference to the 'stone' at line
265, Surly is claiming that venereal disease is all
Mammon will gain
weasel . . . vermin: punning on the ermine fur worn by the steward of
a great lord

Act II Scene iv

The cozeners are exultant in their success, and apparently unaware
that Surly ('Monsieur Caution') is on to their trick. It is a hasty con-
ference, like all the cozeners' meetings once the gulls start arriving.

NOTES AND GLOSSARY:
a gold-end-man: one who trades in scraps of gold

Act II Scene v

Ananias, 'my Anabaptist' as Subtle calls him, now arrives.
Anabaptists, who arose in the Reformation in the sixteenth century,
were the most extreme of Puritan sects in their exclusiveness and in
their refusal to acknowledge any authority but their own conclusions
based on the Bible. Like the three cozeners in their republic and
Mammon in his greed they deny all outside authority. For them Subtle
takes off his alchemist's robe and wears the doctor's gown of black
which will be least offensive to Puritan feelings. He adopts a 'new
tune, new gesture, but old language' (line 27) for them. It is the same
alchemical cant, because the Puritans are also after the philosopher's
stone to give power to their community. Ananias is an agent of the
community living in the Netherlands, the 'exiled brethren' of
Amsterdam, who were at this time preparing to sail to America to set
up a new society there, free from the laws of the ungodly nations of
Europe. Ananias's faith makes his 'brethren' a republic like that of
the cozeners. He would cheat anyone who is not one of the brethren.

Subtle's exchange with Ananias is another chance for him to display
his powers of canting, and to expose the limitations of the Puritan
mentality. He plays Ananias like a hooked fish, to 'make 'hem haste
towards their gulling more' (line 88). The gull is sent off to fetch his
superior with more money.

NOTES AND GLOSSARY:
All's heathen but the Hebrew: since the New Testament was written
in Greek, Ananias is showing his ignorance
A very fugitive: because mercury is liquid and difficult to handle,
it was called the runaway servant in alchemical
jargon. It is a quality which suits Face

Act II Scene vi

Ananias's departure makes room for Drugger to return with more money. Drugger, as we learn at the end of the scene (lines 82-3) actually returned only to ask for a cure for worms in his stomach. But the cozeners don't let him off so lightly. He does in fact get some return for his cash, the contemptibly feeble 'device' contrived out of his name to hang up over his shop door. The sign is a 'mystery' only for feeble minds, and a 'hieroglyphic' which incorporates the name of an astrologer and alchemist whom Queen Elizabeth I (1534-1603) used to employ. The reference to John Dee (1527-1608) in line 20 would have been familiar to all Jonson's original audience. He died only two years before the play was first staged, in 1608. At his death he was still regarded with respect, despite the activities of others of the same sort, of whom Edward Kelley (1555-1595)—he is mentioned at IV.i.90—and Simon Forman (1552-1611) were the best known. Laws passed in 1403 and 1541 had forbidden alchemical experiments. Necromancy or magic was also banned by law. But astrology as Dee practised it was not illegal.

In return for the sign over his shop Drugger pays out one gold piece and one pipeful of tobacco. Tobacco was a new fashion, only recently discovered by the first American colonists. Even in Jonson's lifetime there were several attempts to ban it. It was a very expensive fashion. Face and Subtle however see more profit in Drugger's promise of a new pair of clients, Kastril and his sister, the rich and sexy young widow Pliant. Face and Subtle see her as a double gain: 'We'll e'en draw lots, and he that fails shall have/The more in good, the other has in tail'. Sexual greed is more urgent even than greed for money. What Dame Pliant may offer 'in tail' (entail, i.e. in inheritance) will more than outweigh her wealth. Sex however raises the question of the 'doll' the cozeners have in common, so Act II ends with Subtle and Face plotting to deceive the third member of the venture, who is hardly in a position to share in this new kind of loot.

NOTES AND GLOSSARY:

the balance: the zodiacal sign Libra, commonly used by shopkeepers

a *bona roba*:   (*Latin*) a well-dressed girl, a courtesan

she wears/A hood: unfashionable at this time. It is mentioned at V.ii.22

so light/She may want grains: an extension of the pun on 'entail'. She may be so lacking in virtue that she will be worthless in dowry

Act III Scene i

Act III opens with more cant, this time the language of the exiled and sanctified brethren. Where Ananias is gloomily hostile to the 'heathen' pretences of Subtle the alchemist, Tribulation the elder, a leader of the brethren, replies with sophistries. The younger, Ananias, is the extremist. The older, Tribulation, is the politician. Their ends, power for the brethren, justify illegal means (line 11) of getting power. They need Subtle's art 'for the restoring of the silenced saints' (the Puritan clergy forbidden by the government to hold church services). That end 'ne'er will be, but by the Philosopher's Stone' (lines 38-9). *Aurum potabile,* a phrase which technically meant liquid gold, the elixir of life, but which commonly meant a bribe, is all that will move governments to sympathise with the Puritans. So with this piece of specious self-justification from Tribulation in the street—a parallel to Mammon's persuasion of Surly in the street at the beginning of Act II—the Puritans open Act III and come to the house of gulling in a fitting frame of mind.

NOTES AND GLOSSARY:

the Separation: the brotherhood of 'saints' who live separated from the rest of society in order to preserve their sanctity

we must give: Tribulation means they must bend their principles. In fact he is 'giving' money to the cozeners, the stirrers of humours (line 29)

Act III Scene ii

Subtle welcomes the Puritans with a reference to time. They have returned in exactly the one hour they promised. The time is now noon, the middle of the day and of the play. Subtle provokes more by-play with Puritan sensitivities. When Ananias objects to the word 'mass' as a Catholic and therefore objectionable word, Subtle promptly refers to 'massy gold' (line 45). His speech (lines 69-82) emphasises the hypocrisy of the Puritans at the same time as it makes clear how they think they are gulling him. He taunts them while he tempts them. He promises them the stone in about a fortnight, the length of time which Face at I.i.188 had predicted they could safely have the house before its owner returned. A final twist emphasises the double-think of the Puritans when they consider forging money and conclude that although 'coining' (counterfeiting) is not lawful, 'casting' (the act of coining) is. The whole body of the brethren will have to confirm such a piece of double-think.

NOTES AND GLOSSARY:

wood: a crowd. Subtle is punning on the Latin *silva,* a wood, which metaphorically also meant a crowd. The Latin term suggests that his interest in the Puritans is in their silver

The third examination: the assaying of gold involved three stages of tests

Act III Scene iii

Face reports that Surly did not turn up at the meeting place but that, instead, he has snared a Spanish nobleman. This 'Don' has come to the Blackfriars for a 'bath' (line 16), that is, a cure for venereal disease, and a whore. Subtle's alchemical bath and Dol will supply his desires. As the three cozeners talk their joy over their profits comes out in the exultant word-play. Dol is 'our castle, our cinqueport [a type of fortification], Our Dover pier' (lines 18-19). Dol herself picks up the military image with her first line, 'say, Lord General, how fares our camp?' which is a parody of the opening line from Kyd's *The Spanish Tragedy,* a play famous since 1588. Jonson himself once acted the lead in this play, which is referred to again later at IV.vii.71. The three cozeners are soldiers 'entrenched . . . against a world' by their 'discipline'. In view of the earlier quarrel between Subtle and Face, and their more recent agreement to cut Dol out of the deal over Dame Pliant, this is ironical.

NOTES AND GLOSSARY:

costive cheater: they see Surly as clearly as he sees them. He is a cozener too. His 'humour' is dry and surly because he is constipated ('costive')

God's gift: 'Dol' is short for Dorothea which in Greek means a gift of God

these festival days: an allusion to the performance of plays on feast days. The lesser gulls are too mean to dress themselves in the expensive costumes appropriate to festivals

in my circle: in the necromancer's magic circle; in this case the round promenade area of the Temple where Face was to meet Surly

Act III Scene iv

The number of gulls is now increasing so that several arrive at once. Dapper comes for his meeting with the 'Queen of Faery' at the same time as Drugger returns with the new gull Kastril. The 'angry boy' wants to be a fashionable gallant (line 50), living it up with duelling and smoking. He gets tobacco from Drugger. He comes to Subtle for lessons in how to conduct the quarrel which leads up to a duel. Duelling in fact, being illegal, was a mark of extreme bravado. From a higher basis than Dapper, being a country landowner with an income of £1,500 a year (line 15), Kastril wants to achieve his highest ambition, to live by his wits. Face has fun with all three gulls, Dapper, Kastril and Drugger, before sending the latter two off to fetch more loot and Dame Pliant, and thus leave the coast clear for the gulling of Dapper.

NOTES AND GLOSSARY:

a right line: Face uses geometry as the language of duelling: later (IV.ii.21-9) Subtle uses terms from grammar and rhetoric

a cast commander: an officer who has been dismissed from the army

when your land is gone: Gold needs no looking after compared with land. Lazy landowners at this time were selling land and moving to London to spend the proceeds

for the waterwork: all London property owners had to pay for a new water conduit, a system of water pipes, begun in April 1609, completed 1613

Edward shillings: it was worth knowing the dates of coins, since from 1543 on the metals were regularly debased

---

Act III Scene v

For the gulling of Dapper, Subtle and Dol both put on a new disguise. Subtle speaks in comic rhymes. There is an echo in this scene, where Dapper is blindfolded and manhandled, of the way Falstaff is gulled in Shakespeare's *Merry Wives of Windsor* (1599), and perhaps behind both lie the traditional English folk games in which the Queen of Faery belongs. This manhandling is an inversion of the tradition, a misuse of it comparable to the cozener's misuse of language, since it is done purely to rob Dapper of his cash. Subtle and Dol evidently enjoy it, though, enough to forget the time and the queue of gulls waiting to be robbed. Mammon arrives, and they need to change clothes once more for him. So Face puts on Ulen's (that is the alchemist's assistant's) robe again so that he can keep Mammon waiting at the door while Subtle bundles Dapper off to the toilet, still blindfolded and with a gag of gingerbread in his mouth. He is told he must wait patiently there, although 'the fumigation's somewhat strong' (line 81), till his aunt the Queen is ready for him again. As it happens he has to stay there a full two hours because the pressure of events makes the cozeners forget all about him till his cries bring him back to their memory. Audiences seeing the play on stage tend to forget about him likewise.

Act III ends with more victims than ever set up and no single piece of gulling complete. There is also the time-bomb of Surly. Moreover since the cozeners have already been hard pressed to keep the gulls apart from one another, the risk of a log-jam is increasing. Overwhelmed by the number of people whose greed makes them gullible, the cozeners are getting into trouble through their own greed. The pace of events is heating up. Act IV holds the promise of several crises.

NOTES AND GLOSSARY:

cittern: a kind of guitar

equivocate: the trick practised by Jesuits when questioned by the government, often under torture. Since it was unchristian to tell lies, they developed the art of telling half-truths and evasions

Act IV Scene i

The new act opens with Mammon, the chief gull, being set up for his crisis. Projection for the stone is reaching its climax. Dol tempts his sexual appetite as a trap to ensure his downfall. Face warns him to avoid mentioning holy matters because that will set Dol talking and reveal to the alchemist that Mammon is less pure than he pretends to be. They have Mammon perfectly poised for a self-induced downfall. When he directs his flattery at Dol, in the belief that she is a great lady, the proof of his gullibility is complete. Dol's answers to him are ambiguous—she is no lady; she lacks the trappings of honour; she has been compared to great princes (Mammon has just made the comparison himself). Face emphasises this double talk by giggling at her replies till he has to go away to laugh properly. We then remain in suspense through the rest of what Mammon thinks is his seduction of Dol. We watch him fool himself and wait for the slip into 'controversy' which will set Dol off, spouting cant quotations from Broughton. He survives precariously, painting his picture of unbounded appetite in a 'free state' (line 156), until Face sends them both away for the seduction to take its course, or for Mammon to think it will.

NOTES AND GLOSSARY:

concumber: fornicate. The word, which sounds fairly polite in Latin, is borrowed from Juvenal

guinea bird: prostitute; a brightly coloured fowl and a girl who can be bought for a gold coin

Kelley:	employed as an alchemist by the German Emperor; partner of John Dee (II.vi.20)

Act IV Scene ii

This scene opens with another attempt at bargaining between Subtle and Face over the new client, Dame Pliant. The two cozeners are totally different personalities. When Face, still laughing over Dol's gulling of Mammon, appeals to Subtle to share the joke, Subtle's answer is a curt and hostile 'yes' and a reminder that there is business waiting to be done. He is loud and humourless where Face is soft-spoken and ready to stop work and enjoy the fun. Subtle takes the deceptions seriously. Face enjoys them, and is ready to change at a moment's inspiration. In the opening scene of the play Subtle boasted of his role while Face ridiculed it. In IV.vii, Face twice has to prod Subtle into action to save the situation. At the end of the play we shall see Face adapting his role back to that of Jeremy the butler while Subtle cannot change and has to flee. He is not so subtle in the end as Face. In this scene however he is still 'sovereign' of the great deception and so he is the one to get the first try at Dame Pliant.

First, though, he has to gull her brother. He does so with more dazzling words, a mock grammar of duelling terms as if quarreling was a formal exercise like writing. Then he turns to kissing the sister, on the pretext of examining her face and hand to tell her fortune. He uses sexual innuendos (the *mons veneris* is on the hand, but the name is also given to the swelling over the female sexual organ; the *junctura annularis* is also a sexual allusion). Language is a disguise for many things. Then Face enters, dressed in his military costume, to have his turn with the lady. He too kisses her and uses sexual innuendo. 'I shall be proud to know you, lady' means that he will be on heat (proud was the word used for animals when they are sexually receptive) to 'know' her sexually. When the girl distracts her brother's attention for a moment Face takes the opportunity to whisper to Subtle that the Spanish Don has arrived. So Subtle takes them off for half an hour's studying while Face prepares to tackle the Spaniard.

NOTES AND GLOSSARY:

a Bonibell:	a beauty
terrae Fili:	*(Latin)* a son of the earth, a peasant. Subtle mistranslates the term for Kastril, suggesting it means a young landowner. He is mocking Kastril's habit of calling everyone 'boy', too
a myrobalane:	a sugared plum
kuss:	Kastril's country pronunciation of 'kiss' (also in 'suster')

Act IV Scene iii

The two rogues meet briefly to decide the question of who shall have Dame Pliant. Subtle threatens Face in case he intends to 'rebel' against their republic. Face offers to compensate Subtle with some of his share of the loot if he can have the girl. Then Surly enters, dressed like a Spanish nobleman with a huge ruff around his neck, looking as if his head was on a plate, as Subtle unflatteringly describes him. The dress is so absurd that the audience will see it is Surly, even though Face and Subtle do not—a good example of where Jonson draws the line in the.quest for realism and makes use of theatrical convention.

The disguised Surly is now gulling the gullers. Like them he uses language for deceit, not to reveal truth. His Spanish is correct—Jonson probably took it from a phrasebook—and it allows Surly to posture while Face and Subtle make fools of themselves insulting him to his face, in the belief that he cannot understand their for once open language. For once they are speaking the truth. 'You shall/Be cozened, Diego', Subtle tells him, and Face repeats the word. They do, however, have a practical problem in cozening the Spaniard. He has come for a whore, and Dol is still busy with Sir Epicure. The greed of the cozeners is making them take on more than they can manage. Face then thinks of Dame Pliant. If the Spaniard has her it won't be much loss since she is a widow and no virgin. The whole 'venture' will be at risk if somebody is not provided for the Don. As Face says in an ironically commercial metaphor, 'The credit of our house too is engaged'. They will lose their reputation as honest merchants if they fail to deliver the goods. They then bargain briefly, Subtle trying to bring back Face's offer of a share in his part of the loot in return for the girl, and Face insisting on equal shares, 'the common cause'. Otherwise he will tell Dol of the bargaining—a reminder that their cause is not common to all three of the partners. Subtle, who earlier had indignantly denied Face's assertion that he was too old for sex with Dame Pliant, now claims that he is after all too old. But, when Face calls his bluff and shouts for Dol to come, he reluctantly agrees and they shake hands to seal their new bargain. The disguised Surly is then taken off to meet Dame Pliant, and Subtle goes off with him swearing revenge on Face for the bad bargain into which he has blackmailed Subtle.

NOTES AND GLOSSARY:

composition:	financial settlement
Entiendo:	*(Spanish)* I understand. Surly is saying he knows they plan to cozen him. They think he says he 'intends' to be cozened

rampant:	Surly has been called a lion at line 46. 'Rampant' is a term in heraldry, signifying a beast rearing up ready to attack
flawed and tawed:	flayed and dressed like leather

Act IV Scene iv

The scene begins with first Face and then Subtle persuading Kastril and Dame Pliant into the idea of her marrying a Spanish Count. There is some by-play between the rogues. Face has rushed off to tell Dame Pliant of the new plan before Subtle can change his mind, so when Subtle begins his flowery speech about her 'honorable fortune' (line 19), Face interrupts to say it is unnecessary. Subtle sarcastically replies 'Still, my scarce worshipful Captain, you can keep/No secret', a statement which of course has much more meaning for Face than for Dame Pliant or her brother. When the girl objects to the idea of a Spanish husband first Kastril attempts to persuade her by threatening to kick her, then Subtle and Face together offer her smoother persuasions. So the disguised Surly is introduced to his intended whore, and Kastril's gulling has progressed a step further. There is a sexual pun in Subtle's assurance to him that he will 'be brother/To a great Count'.

NOTES AND GLOSSARY:

nick:	a pun on the female sexual organ
this is my scheme:	the paper on which Subtle has drawn Pliant's horoscope
eighty-eight:	1588, the year of the Spanish Armada's unsuccessful attempt to invade England
cry strawberries:	sell fruit in the market-place because her reputation andyed and dressed like leather

Act IV Scene v

Mammon now reappears. Dol was told by Face to start her talking fit as Subtle instructed at IV.iv.83, and she now erupts on stage spouting Broughton, while Mammon in agony begs her to stop. Face, back in his role as Ulen the alchemist's assistant, prepares Mammon for the final blow, and there is a crescendo of noise as Mammon and Face confer together over the noise of Dol's recitation. Then Subtle arrives to confront Mammon with the evidence of his greed in the person of Dol. This is the planned climax of the alchemical gulling. Subtle's parody of Christian reproof against sinners prepares us for the explosion which destroys Mammon's hopes of getting the stone. In a scene of frantic activity, one of the few in which all three of the conspirators appear together, Subtle pretends to faint in horror at the disastrous consequences of Mammon's lack of propriety. A knock on the door (which gull this time?) is turned to advantage by Face, who pretends it is Dol's brother and hurries Mammon out the back way. The trio briefly celebrate their success before Face has to change costume again, ready to complete the gulling of the Spaniard. The main gulling is complete, the rest are poised for equal success.

NOTES AND GLOSSARY:

a fifth monarchy: the Bible predicted a kingdom of Christ and the saints in succession to the four great kingdoms on earth, Assyria, Persia, Greece and Rome. The idea of Mammon establishing it is in complete contrast to his 'free state' of IV.i.156.

Act IV Scene vi

We now see how far from success the second main gulling plan is, and how premature are Subtle's and Face's congratulations. Surly has shed his disguise and is telling Dame Pliant the truth. He sees that his own best hope lies in marrying the Dame not as a Spaniard but as himself. By revealing the 'republic' of deceivers he hopes to 'claim some interest' in Dame Pliant's love for her rescuer. He is as greedy a rogue as the venture tripartite rogues. But at this point he is doing the more successful gulling by telling the truth. The scene ends with him unmasking and confronting both Subtle and Face with the fact that he has unmasked them.

NOTES AND GLOSSARY:

I will make your pockets so: picking the gull's pockets was Dol's job. Subtle is doing what Face suggested at IV.v.109, in Dol's absence

. . . wherewith you cheat abroad in taverns: Surly gives some details of how Face and Subtle perform their tricks

Act IV Scene vii

Face is the quick-witted partner. Before Surly has spoken ten lines of his triumphant abuse Face steals away to get Kastril. He brings him in now to confront Surly and practise his new learning in the art of picking quarrels. Kastril does it, very clumsily, of course, but well enough to stop Surly. Kastril is the lady's brother, and too well cozened by Face and Subtle for Surly to be able to convince him that he is being gulled. When more gulls appear to keep the appointments made earlier Face uses them to drive Surly away. Abel Drugger adds his gullible testimony, and Ananias, the younger Puritan, reacts predictably to Surly's Spanish clothes. For Ananias they make him both a hated Catholic and an extravagant dresser. 'That ruff of pride/About thy neck betrays thee' (lines 51-2) he tells Surly. 'Thou look'st like Antichrist in that lewd hat ' (line 55). So Surly is driven away from Dame Pliant by a flock of gulls.

While Kastril sees Surly off the premises Face takes advantage of Drugger's arrival to ask him if he can obtain some Spanish clothes. With Surly unmasked the rogues have still to find the Spanish Count promised to Kastril as a husband for Dame Pliant. Meanwhile Subtle deals with Ananias. He has come to confirm what Subtle expected, that the Puritan brethren are hypocritical enough, and ready enough, to scorn the law and decide that coining money is acceptable. In their own private state 'casting of money is most lawful'. Subtle sends them off, gathering his wits enough to explain that the Spaniard was a spy. Face reproves him for his slowness: 'Thou art so down upon the least disaster!/How would'st thou ha done if I had not helped thee out?' (lines 93-4). He also checks Subtle's attempt to renegotiate the bargain over Dame Pliant, and Subtle again mutters that in their republic Face is acting like a tyrant. Tyrants should have even less of a place in a republic than in a monarchy. Face replies that he is sticking to the law of their treaty—'Strict for my right' (line 106). He reasserts the treaty just as the biggest danger of all begins to loom over them.

Act IV, an act of high risk and high achievement for the 'household rogues', ends with Dol's news that the owner of the house has returned, against all their expectations, and is outside the door. The outside world is threatening their little republic, their 'citadel', quite as much as the internal quarrels. In the outside world the plague has abated. Subtle accuses Face of miscalculating, and is sarcastic about Face's excuse. But he still relies on Face's quick wit to rescue them, and his trust is not misplaced. Face proposes to shave off his new beard and return to his old shape as Jeremy the butler. In that role he will hold off his master while Subtle and Dol escape. They will share the loot hidden in the cellar later, when they meet at 'Ratcliff', a meeting house downriver in Stepney.

NOTES AND GLOSSARY:

the unclean birds: a visit by strange birds with neck feathers like Spanish ruffs in 1586 (not 1577) was thought to be an omen. Ananias uses the term again at V.ii.47

a brokerly slave: a minor go-between. Drugger arrives finally with the damask suit which Face has kept asking for, only to be sent off again for a Spanish suit

Act V Scene i

Lovewit enters the play for the first time in Act V, bringing the world with him. His neighbours report the truth to him, that many people have been visiting his house in his absence. Face, of course, is skilled at obscuring the truth, but his master is not so readily gulled as the other victims. His first reaction to what his neighbours tell him is not anger but amused puzzlement. The situation sounds interesting. As he says, 'I love a teeming wit as I love my nourishment'. Face is the right kind of provider for such a man, but as partner rather than as cozener.

NOTES AND GLOSSARY:
Pimlico: a popular tavern
downward: definitely

Act V Scene ii

Face is also the man to outface the testimony of Lovewit's neighbours. The cat had the plague, he tells his master, and so he locked up the house. Nobody passed in or out. So smoothly does he give his assurances (he has lots of 'face') that the neighbours subside into a confused mumbling. Face is on the point of convincing Lovewit that all is well. But then a new crisis looms which makes even Face feel despair. 'What shall I do?/Nothing's more wretched than a guilty conscience', he says in an aside. Surly has been to tell Mammon how he was gulled, and both are returning to the scene of the crime for revenge.

NOTES AND GLOSSARY:
the cat: in fact bubonic plague, carried by a rat-flea, does not infect animals as it does human beings
seen double/Through the black pot: been confused by drinking alcohol

Act V Scene iii

The revengers appear, with Mammon echoing to Surly what Subtle had said to Face. Surly is tyrannising over Mammon for being so gullible, and Mammon wants to pay off his humiliation on the cozeners. They hammer on the door while Lovewit stands by amazed at this new turn of events. Face steps forward to outflank them, knowing that without his beard they will see him only as the butler whose clothes he is dressed in. He first tries exactly the trick he had just used against the neighbours, bland contradiction. They say one thing, he coolly maintains the opposite, with such a modestly honest air that they too begin to doubt themselves. But Surly's mind is a suspicious one. He will not be so easily convinced that he is mistaken. He takes Mammon off, threatening to return with law officers to force an entry and find the evidence he is sure is in the house.

After that the gulls turn up thick and fast. First Kastril, who has also been shown his foolishness by Surly, storms in. Then the Puritans, similarly enlightened. Lovewit and his butler stand silently by while the gulls shout and beat on the door. Twice Lovewit tries to speak to the gulls, first to Surly (line 24), then to the second group (line 52), but they all brush past him. Face still tries to brazen it out, even though the neighbours are claiming that some of the angry gulls were among the visitors they had seen when the house was supposed to be locked up. But then comes the final blow, the voice last heard right back in III.v. It is Dapper, still locked in the toilet, his gingerbread gag melted in his mouth, crying plaintively that his aunt, the Queen of Faery, is neglecting him. Subtle is also heard trying to quieten him. Face cannot check his bitter comment on hearing Subtle's voice, and on hearing that Lovewit realises that Face must have the answer to all these amazing events. He demands 'The truth, the shortest way' (line 74).

So Face is driven to twist yet again. He will enter a new league with his master in place of the old venture with Dol and Subtle. The widow Pliant will be a bribe to make the league worth Lovewit's while. Face even maintains that it will give Lovewit the benefits Mammon had hoped for from the philosopher's stone. 'It will make you seven years younger, and a rich one' (line 86) he tells Lovewit. A rich gull? Face suggests that it is sex, not the stone, which provides youth, sexual potency, and money. Lovewit is human too. He will fall for Face's bribe out of a greed less mountainous than Mammon's but made of the same material.

NOTES AND GLOSSARY:

lights:	entrails. Face is punning on Mammon's pet name for Ulen, 'lungs'
a new face:	an unconscious pun by Surly. He sees Face as a stranger
wild-fowl:	an echo of Ananias's 'unclean birds', and also a reference to Kastril and to the gulls generally

Act V Scene iv

Scene iv moves inside the house to where Subtle is coping with the confused Dapper, now out of the toilet. Face joins them. He has shaved off his beard to make himself into Jeremy again, and not like the Captain Face whom Dapper knew, but his voice is the same, and since Dapper is still blindfolded he cannot see the transformation. Subtle does not untie the blindfold until Face has gone again.

Despite his readiness to go ahead with the gulling of Dapper in this scene, Subtle is near the end of his tether. When Face brings him reassurance over Lovewit's arrival, he is so relieved that he is ready to burst into song in praise of 'Face so famous, the precious king/Of present [quick] wits'. Where Subtle earlier had been king to Face's general, and had accused Face of playing the tyrant, now he welcomes Face's sovereignty. He admits to having 'dwindled' in size on hearing the fuss outside the door, a remarkably accurate word for the shrinking stature of the puffed-up reciter of cant. His transformation is to shrink from his pretended sovereignty to his normal meanness. From now on Face orders Subtle to do things where before Subtle gave the orders.

Dapper is gulled by Dol and Subtle and dismissed in some haste. Face then returns with the news that Drugger has brought the new suit of Spanish clothes, presumably borrowed as Face had suggested from a company of actors. He refers to them at IV.vii.71, and here at line 68, as belonging to Hieronymo, the hero of *The Spanish Tragedy*. Face orders Subtle to collect them from Drugger and send the poor gull off again for a priest to perform the marriage with Dame Pliant. Face then takes the clothes, pretending that he is fulfilling the bargain with Subtle, whereby he would be the one to marry the widow. In reality, of course, he needs them for his master in order to fulfil the new bargain with him. Subtle mentions his bargain apologetically to Dol, once Face has left, and she replies sullenly 'Tis direct/Against our articles', contrary to the terms of the original indenture tripartite. They agree to break off from Face, and Dol promises to steal as much as she can from Dame Pliant. Subtle proposes that instead of heading east down-river to the agreed rendezvous at Ratcliff in Stepney they should go in the opposite direction to Brentford. The betrayal has become mutual.

Face returns to announce that the priest has come, and orders Subtle to send Drugger away again to wash himself ready for his presumed marriage with the widow. They count up their loot, which Subtle and Dol have packed up in cases ready for their escape from the house. Face takes the keys of the cases, and then triumphantly declares that he will keep them for himself and his new partner Lovewit. He insultingly addresses Subtle by his pretended title of 'Doctor' and mocks his claim to be able to tell the future by asserting (falsely) that he himself had sent for Lovewit. 'For all your figures' (the casting of horoscopes to predict the future, line 128) Subtle did not foresee this breach in the indenture tripartite. All that Subtle and

Dol will be allowed to escape with is the clothing they have on. They must leave with little more than they had when they first met Jeremy the butler. Face mockingly offers to supply Dol with letters of introduction to famous brothel-keepers, and that is all. The two gulled rogues—the last of the long sequence of gulls—have no time even to curse Face as they hear the law officers, summoned by Surly and Mammon, hammering at the door. So they flee out by the back door in the same furtive way as they originally entered.

NOTES AND GLOSSARY:

wriggle: shuffle forward on your knees

fly: probably a flea, since it feeds on blood

heaven and hell: two Westminster taverns

we'll fit him: an echo of a famous line from *The Spanish Tragedy* where Hieronymo swears revenge

a-billing: kissing; literally of birds, touching bills. Face is asserting that his partners have become birds for the plucking, gulls like all their victims

smock-rampant: a smock was a woman's undergarment. Rampant here means the same as at IV.iii.57

Act V Scene v

The final scene begins with Lovewit in the Hieronymo costume answering the hammering on his door. His wearing of the costume indicates that he has fully accepted Face's deal and is willing to act as Face's partner in the final gulling. Face arrives, checks that the marriage between Lovewit and Dame Pliant has been performed, whips off Lovewit's costume so that he can resume his role as master of the house, and opens the door just in time to prevent Surly and the others from smashing it down. The gulls all tumble in together, shouting for revenge on the three cozeners, one of whom has just let them in and whom they fail to recognise once again. Lovewit and Face stand happily by, as the gulls fall over one another in their impatience. Then Lovewit asks the law officers who have come in with them to check their 'violence' (line 17), as an honest householder should. Lovewit is acting a deception quite as thorough as those of Subtle and Face earlier in the play. He is the innocent owner whose privacy is being violated by madmen. He steers close to the truth in his speech (lines 26-37), just close enough to halt the gulls and emphasise the contrast between his calm and their fury. His control of the situation is perfect. He lets Mammon and the Puritans charge off to search the house before announcing calmly what they will find. He mentions Dame Pliant, and lets her brother charge off in search of her before announcing to the one remaining gull, Surly, that he has married her for himself. Thus Surly, the cleverest of the gulls, is the last to hear of his loss. Lovewit mocks him for his slowness, especially in the sexual sense. The widow blamed him because he 'did nothing'. Lovewit with his ancient weapon was quicker.

Mammon returns counting his losses. They include £90 in cash, plus all the metal goods he had delivered to the house in the expectation that they would be turned into gold. Lovewit denies him even the chance of rescuing the metal which he has discovered stored in the cellar. The house's owner will keep it unless Mammon is prepared to produce a certificate to prove that he has been gulled out of it. That would be the very last twist of humiliation for Mammon's pride, and he finally admits total defeat. Surly likewise admits defeat, picking up Lovewit's account of how Dame Pliant disliked his conduct and recognising that it was 'that same foolish vice of honesty' (line 84) which has beaten him. Instead of following his usual practice of cozening he had spoken the truth to Dame Pliant, and as a result has lost the prize. A final turn of Jonson's knife has them both leaving the stage telling the sympathetic Face, now disguised of course as Jeremy, that if they ever catch Face they will beat him. Face farewells them saying innocently that he thought the cozeners were 'honest as myself' (line 89). The gulls have never learned to see the truth through Face's deceptions.

Lovewit's retention of Mammon's goods is a trick the Puritans are likely to suffer from as well. They return to the stage preparing 'to bear away the portion of the righteous / Out of this den of thieves' (lines 92-3). But they have proved themselves far from righteous, and Lovewit underlines the point by telling them that the goods in the cellar belong not to God but Mammon. Their worldliness is to be punished by the loss of their worldly goods. Lovewit promises to send them to join the rest of the brethren in exile in Amsterdam, away from the country whose laws they ignore.

Drugger is dismissed even more smartly than the Puritans. Face twists his tail by telling him he spent too long washing his face in preparation for his marriage to Dame Pliant. Like poor Dapper, Drugger never learns that he has been gulled. These two are merely foolish. The higher intensity of greed belongs to Mammon, the Puritans and Surly, and they suffer the greater punishment of knowing they have been tricked.

And that leaves only Kastril to deal with. He enters dragging in his sister and cursing her because she has married a gentleman of lower rank than a knight, a 'dubbed boy' (line 127). Lovewit, presumably forewarned of Kastril's ambitions by Face, rises to the occasion. He quarrels with Kastril with a bravado that commands Kastril's admiration. He claims Dame Pliant as his 'dove' and challenges her brother to 'stoop' (that is, to dive on her) like the birds of prey which his name indicates, at his peril. Kastril, delighted at such clever quarreling, changes his tune from anger to appeasement. If Lovewit is capable of smoking and drinking as well as quarreling, Kastril will even hand over his sister with a new dowry. Lovewit, of course, does have tobacco ready in the house. It was delivered by poor Drugger. Face's quick wits are capable of turning the smallest piece of fortune to good advantage. His resourcefulness makes him the perfect partner. Thus Lovewit the master agrees (line 143) to be ruled by his servant. This is the final inversion of the play. Lovewit can gull all the gulls, including Kastril, but his mastery comes from his servant.

In the end, therefore, although Lovewit starts to speak the Epilogue (lines 146-65), he soon hands it over to Face. Both of them have to apologise to the audience for their deceit and the fact that they have got away with all the loot. The way they do it is Jonson's final declaration of his intention in his comedy. First Lovewit apologises for his share in the cozening. He declares that Face has given him so much that it would be ungrateful not to 'help his fortune', that is, share the loot with him, even though the price is a little dishonesty—'at some small strain / Of his own candour' (lines 151-2). And then he turns directly to the audience and rephrases the apology in the terms of comic theory. The transformation Mammon had expected from the philosopher's stone has come to Lovewit through Dame Pliant ('a young wife') and his servant ('a good brain'). Face has ended up not as Mammon's or Subtle's 'lungs' but as Lovewit's 'brain', the role for which he is best fitted. This transformation of Lovewit has altered his character. He has not acted with consistency in the stock character of the old man, the *senex* or old gull of Latin comedy. Lovewit apologises 'if I have outstripped / An old man's gravity, or strict canon' of comic theory. With Dame Pliant in his bed and her money in his coffers he can afford to.

Face also apologises for his transformation, from being an equal partner of the cozening trio to the role famous in classical comedy, the clever servant. 'Yet 'twas *decorum*', he adds. It was proper, it was the correct adjustment to make. In this last scene Face has forsaken his place in the 'free republic' of thieves and cozeners and returned to his former place as his master's loyal servant. What more proper thing could he do than that? 'Decorum', however, also means artistic propriety, the sense of fitness which makes the playwright deal out the rewards and punishments which match the characters and their actions in the play. Face is claiming that it was right for him to betray the republicans and that justice has been done by his return to his master's service.

It is not for Face to be his own judge, of course, especially when an audience is there to sit in judgement on the whole play. Face therefore ends the Epilogue with an appeal to the jury he is addressing. 'I put myself / On you that are my country [the jury in my trial]', he declares. And 'if you do quit (aquit) me', he continues, 'this pelf' [this sordid loot] will be at the audience's service for more performances. The play is a trial with the playwright as prosecuting council and the audience as jury. The folly of the gullible is on show. In the words which ended the Prologue,

> They are so natural follies, but so shown
> As even the doers may see, and yet not own.

NOTES AND GLOSSARY:

A kind of choughs: Mammon completes the bird imagery by labelling the cozeners as eaters of carrion

Harry Nicholas: leader of the Anabaptist 'family of love', he lived from 1502 to 1580

mammet: puppet

Part 3

Commentary

The plot

Jonson's faith in classical models made him always aim to preserve the unities of action, space and time in his plays. It was a principle inflated out of an observation by Aristotle in the *Poetics* that, if they are to be realistic, plays cannot afford to cover too long a time span or too many separate localities. The number of characters have to be limited to those who are relevant to the main story, and the story itself cannot spread beyond a single 'action'. Jonson's own theory set realism very high, and he accordingly used Aristotle's observations as his own organising principle. *The Alchemist* takes place in the daylight hours of a single day, from a little before 9 a.m. till about 5 p.m., in and around one locality, Lovewit's house. Everything that happens in the course of these eight hours is a direct consequence of the cozeners' plans to gull the neighbourhood.

All the scenes in the play are located on one side or the other of the main door in Lovewit's house. The door is a visual focus for the entry or exit of the gulls into the 'republic' of cozeners, and people are constantly either speaking through the keyhole, being blocked from entry while a hurried change is made on stage, or banging on it demanding to be let in. Other doors also exist to indicate the inner rooms of the house, including Subtle's laboratory and Dapper's lavatory, but Jonson concentrates all the events into the one space adjacent to the main door. He makes no use of other stage areas such as the balcony, or the alcove for 'discovering' displays and set-pieces of the sort which opens his play *Volpone* (1605). Everything is centralised.

Time is measured with similar care. Indications of what time of day it is are given at regular intervals. The quarrel which opens the play takes place at first light. In I.ii Dapper arrives at 9 a.m., and is told to return at 1 p.m. Mammon arrives an hour later, having been expected since sunrise (as Subtle says at I.iv.11-12). Even his greed could not drag him from his comfortable bed too early. Subtle tells Mammon, at II.ii.4, that projection will take place in another three hours, that is, a little after Dapper's return for his 1 p.m. appointment. Face then makes his appointment to meet Surly at the Temple in a half hour, and tells Mammon to return before the projection to meet Dol, in two hours' time, that is, about 12.30. At 11 a.m. Ananias appears, and is told to go away and return in one hour, that is, 12 noon, with more money. His visit and Drugger's have delayed Face, who is now (II.vi.94) late for his appointment with Surly.

In Act III, precisely at noon, Ananias returns as appointed. Face has missed Surly at the Temple in the meantime, but has secured a new gull, as he thinks, in the Spanish Count, who he says will come in an hour. This would be 1 p.m., the time appointed also for Dapper to return. However Dapper arrives first (III.iii). Subtle is now preparing for projection, at the end of the three hours he told Mammon it would take. Surly now appears disguised as the Spaniard (IV.iii.20), presumably a little late because the cozeners have had time to dispose of Dapper arfd make their other dispositions. Subtle declares that projection has been delayed 'this half hour', that is, to 2 p.m. The explosion and the end of the main gulling plot then follows.

Lovewit returns to his house at the end of Act IV at 3 p.m. At V.ii.30 we are told it is not yet 'deep i' the afternoon'. The play twists and turns to its breathless conclusion well before nightfall and the hour when London citizens, including the audience, would expect to go to their dinners. The time-span has been the hours of daylight in an English November, the month when the play was first performed. It fits effortlessly within the length of time Aristotle thought reasonable, a natural or twenty-four hour day.

The unity of action is much more central to the play's artistic success than the other two unities, of time or place. No play has such an intricately woven structure of interlocking events. There is no subplot of the kind Shakespeare used to make parallels and contrasts, and which Jonson used for light relief in *Volpone*. There are no characters peripheral to the central movement of the play as there are in *Bartholomew Fair*. Every character is a cozener or a gull, every action relates to the cozeners' plot. Every twist of the plot is explicable, from Subtle's overbold assumption in IV.vi that Surly will be too weary after his sex with Dame Pliant to notice his pocket being picked, to Dapper being forgotten in the lavatory. The plot structure, like the central imagery of the play, is a marvellously adroit weave of intricate causes and effects. This intricate unity is the most conspicuous feature of the play's artistry.

Realism

Allegiance to the unities was an integral part, though not a central one, of Jonson's theory of art and of comic drama. They were useful for the realism on which his theory of comedy insisted. Realism was necessary because the central function of comedy as he saw it was to be morally educative. For the most direct and powerful impact on an audience realism was vital. The coinage of his imagination had to be recognisable if it was to be valid currency. Drama is the most immediate of all art forms, the form which most directly assaults its audience. Comic realism is the most immediate mode in dramatic form, the one with the most basic and, therefore, the most urgent appeal. As such, its appeal was much broader than the masques which were Jonson's other main artistic vehicle. Masques dealt in visual and verbal allegories, the 'removed mysteries' which only an élite audience at Court might hope to get at. Comic realism was the correct thing to offer the average Londoner.

Having asserted that realism was a useful feature of Jonson's theory, we have of course to admit that it is by no means the same thing as the everyday realism of the cinema or even of the nineteenth-century novel. Modern realism comes close to being an end in itself. Modern novelists accept the precept 'don't tell it, show it', and what is shown often has nothing obvious to tell at all. Jonson felt strongly that his mode of showing must make what he had to tell, his moral point, entirely obvious. So he used realism not as an end in itself but as a means of clarifying his point. The linkages with contemporary reality, in the references to the alchemists Dee and Kelley, the echoes of tricks publicised in current lawsuits, such as the one which gave a precedent for the gulling of Dapper with the Queen of the Faery, these are Jonson's reminders that his story is no fantasy and that his play is a true reflection of human conduct. He made his scene almost painfully local to his first audiences. The Blackfriars was distinguished for its population of magnates (like Mammon) and Puritans, and the other gulls were familiar London types. The summer of 1610 moreover had been a particularly bad time for the plague. Audiences flocking to the Blackfriars theatre, once the number of plague deaths had shrunk enough to allow the theatres to reopen, would all have passed dozens of houses still locked and shuttered, their owners staying away on their country estates till it was safe to return. The play has as local a setting as any ever could have.

Theory

Face, Dol and Subtle have been identified as representations of respectively, the World, the Flesh, and the Devil. Subtle with his black art, his collier's complexion and his misuse of language, is in all respects the antithesis of Christian virtue. He transforms honest learning and truth in words into their opposites. His work is devilish. Dol, a piece of 'common' property, is likewise the antithesis of virtue, a seducer, using the flesh to transform the mind. And Face is the man of the world who completes the pattern of temptations which the Book of Common Prayer calls the Word, the Flesh and the Devil, the features of life on earth which carry mankind to damnation. Worldliness in the person of Face introduces men to the temptations of the flesh in the person of Dol (Surly recognises a brothel when he sees one), and delivers them into the hands of the Devil, in the person of Subtle. The three characters have a poetic and metaphorical function in the play's structure which is discreetly signalled by such hints as the collier reference and which is confirmed by the development of the plot. And yet at the same time as they perform this metaphorical function they are all three realistic human beings.

For Jonson the realism was a matter of detail. What mattered was the metaphorical pattern and the plot, because both contribute directly to his educational aim. Subtle is realistically portrayed. He is exactly the type of certain kinds of actor. He has a dark and pitted complexion, a loud voice and a degree of self-esteem which makes him love to act the role of a master of mysteries. He wears robes which signal a learning and a wisdom he does not possess. He speaks the words which go with the pretence of learning out of totally hypocritical motives ('hypocrite' was the Greek word for an actor). He is used to bluffing his way out of difficulties with noise and bluster. He is not a solitary like Face—he keeps a woman as his partner and helper because he needs constant reassurance that his roles are successful. He demands precedence. He takes the starring roles in the play-scenes the cozeners put on for their gulls. He insists on being king of the republic of tricksters, and grumbles when Face's natural ability puts him in front. And he is not very successful. He lacks Face's quick wit and adaptability. He was starving when Face found him. In all these realistic details Subtle is far more emphatically an individual, a realised human being, than a metaphorical representation of the Devil. Face and Dol have similarly individualised characters. A recognisable humanity in all the cozeners—including Surly and, in the end, Lovewit—is the first necessity for Jonson's purposes in comic drama. They are individuals first and types—representatives of their kind—after.

All human beings are in the end alike. At least, they are enough alike to justify a theory of types and the assumption that individuality is not so extreme that no similarities between human beings can be identified. Jonson's theory of human physiology as based on the humours in the body justified him in identifying human types in relation to the balance of humours. Today we use other theories to identify human types, but the principle is the same. We might put more stress now on individual differences than on patterns of resemblance, but we still accept the necessity of understanding human nature by identifying types of human beings and their characteristic behaviour patterns. Where Jonson differs from modern writers is not in his recognition of individuals and types but in his readiness to intensify the characteristics of the type at the expense of the individual's realism. So his gulls tend to be extreme representatives of their type rather than ordinary representatives. The lesser gulls are types of 'humorous' aberrations. The choleric Kastril, phlegmatic Drugger, sanguine Dame Pliant and melancholic Dapper make a pattern of the four humours. They are all concentrations of the tendencies of their respective types.

Mammon is a concentration of tendencies too, though not of the typology of humours. As the arch-gull he stands as the exemplar of the Seven Deadly Sins. From the sloth of his late arrival to be gulled to the lechery which defeats his greed, he is a concentration of all the sins. Pride, lechery, greed, sloth, gluttony, anger and envy rule his conduct without the least restraint. And the other set of gulls, the Puritans, represent in concentrated form all the vices which Jonson saw as latent in the 'zeal' of small religious sects. They transform reason through language as does Subtle. But where Subtle does it knowingly out of simple greed the Puritans do it hypocritically, twisting words to suit their purposes ('counterfeiting' into 'coining') and blinding themselves to the moral implications of their actions. Their self-righteousness is as immoral as Mammon's greed. It stems from a similar pride in their superiority over other men (pride was the cardinal sin, prompting all the others). Their desire to use the philosopher's stone for their own purposes is just as dangerously ambitious and just as immoral as Mammon's. Even in the way he differentiates the two Puritans Jonson was concentrating the details and displaying the essence of his observations of the type. The ignorantly narrow-minded and prickly young Ananias contrasts neatly with the smoothly diplomatic elder Tribulation Wholesome. Tribulation will be hypocritical and engage in double-think if the means justify his ends. Ananias for all his stubbornness is easily led through his stupidity and his faith in the word of his elders. Between them they cover the whole range of errors which misplaced zeal can lead men into. They are wholly distinct individuals at the same time as they are exemplars of the abuses which Jonson wanted to draw to his audience's attention. They are the 'ambitious Faces of the time' which Jonson mentions in the dedicatory letter to Lady Wroth.

The more such Faces choose to paint themselves (strictly, apply cosmetics as court ladies always did), says Jonson, the less they are 'themselves'. In this statement lies the core of his belief in art as moral. Man is properly a virtuous creature. Surly says at II.iii.279-80 that Mammon is 'a grave sir, a rich, that has no need./A wise sir, too, at other times'. When Original Sin or any of the Seven Deadly Sins rule his conduct he is not his true self. His humours are unbalanced, his sense of his own moral nature is lost and inverted. This inversion is the world of Jonson's art, moral comedy. Its duty is to display the inversion for what it is. Men's manners, he says in the Prologue, are now called humours. Men have lost sight of the essential moral element in human conduct, and excuse their behaviour by labelling their excesses 'humours', as if the physiological basis for their conduct excused and even justified any immorality. In this remarkably early identification of behaviourist psychology Jonson was upholding the traditional social virtues. He was fighting a rearguard action against the individualism which put self before society. The non-moral observation of human activity, seen in Machiavelli (1469-1527) in his books about political action, he saw as a threat to moral and social order. And he had reason. Francis Bacon the philosopher (1561-1626) was already on record quoting approvingly the boast of Machiavelli that he wrote about what men do, not what they ought to do. Individualism and self-interest of the kind which allows Mammon openly to uphold the maxim 'be rich!' was a challenge to everything Jonson valued in human society. It was a challenge which had appeared on many fronts and scored many victories already.

By concentrating his pictures of contemporary 'humours' and vices Jonson saw himself not just holding the mirror up to human nature, but to fallen nature, to those inversions of man's proper self which man most needed to identify and to correct. Dramatic comedy could help that process of identification more powerfully than any other literary form. The story involves characters realistic enough to be identifiable in contemporary life, types identifiable in any variety of human life, and all set in a pattern of humours and of sins so that the points Jonson wanted to tell could be encountered directly, the moral shown, not told. When Face, speaking the Epilogue, offers the audience a bribe—'this pelf' to 'feast you often'—it is the final challenge to his audience's moral sensitivity. More plays? More games? More fun? Is that all the performance has been? Judge for yourself. As the Prologue had put it:

> They are so natural follies, but so shown
> As even the doers may see, and yet not own.

Jonson's target is his audience, not the characters themselves. Whether Mammon or Subtle or Ananias learn from their punishments and reform does not matter, because, ultimately, they are only fictions. The audience is real, and its moral behaviour, its 'manners, now called humours' are what count. So Jonson's aim is not, ultimately, to deliver justice of any kind, legal or poetic, to his characters, but rather to make sure his audience see all the inversions portrayed on stage clearly and learn from them.

Most critics of *The Alchemist* have not taken this point very strongly. In consequence much of the discussion about the play's moral force has centred not on the whole picture of inversion in society but on the ending and Lovewit's success in carrying off all the loot. Alvin Kernan, for instance, states* that the play ends 'with no sense of a better and more stable society having evolved'. Of course not. It is in the audience, not on stage, that improvement must be looked for. C. G. Thayer notes† that since Lovewit is gulled into protecting Face, the play shows that greed and folly are universal. George Parfitt sees it as jungle law‡. So they should, as audience to the play. But they should go further and acknowledge that Jonson is concerned not only to display what men do, but to imply what they ought to do. In *Volpone* he described the aim of art as being not just realistic portrayal but 'to inform men in the best reason of living'. Alan C. Dessen, who thinks that Jonson 'plants the disturbing suggestion that, owing to our culpability, there is only limited hope for improvement in the world outside the theatre'**, is ignoring all Jonson's own declarations of his artistic theory.

Structure

Jonson's deep moral concern for society rather than the individual fits his preference for, and his ability in, comedy more than tragedy. Where tragedy by its nature focuses on the individual character, and requires a single central character to provide the focal point, comedy deals in man as a social being and requires a complex of characters and a pattern of interaction amongst them all. Drama is a form well suited to present the wide variety of human postures. Comedy is in some respects a better means of utilising this feature than tragedy. The moral force of a tragedy to a large extent depends on the audience's sympathy for the individual hero, and their admiration of his conduct. The moral force of a comedy emerges out of a direct assault on the audience. It does not confirm sympathies, it challenges assumptions. The audience must evaluate the events it witnesses, criticise them, and relate these criticisms to its own conduct. So in *The Alchemist* Jonson uses comedy to stimulate his audience's moral awareness. The antisocial self-seeking of his knaves is shown in the way they exploit the fools. The antics of the fools under the guidance of the knaves show their folly. There are no heroes, there is no one central

* *The Cankered Muse,* Yale University Press, page 190.
† *Ben Jonson, Studies in the Plays,* University of Oklahoma Press, page 106.
‡ *Ben Jonson, Public Poet and Private Man,* Dent, page 75.
** *Jonson's Moral Comedy,* Northwestern University Press, page 137.

character. The purpose of the knaves is to use their knowledge of human weaknesses for their personal gain. The purpose of the writer of comedy is to use his knowledge of human weaknesses for social improvement. The knaves do the writer's work for him, but must ultimately be discarded too.

Jonson's comedy, seen from this point of view, is more pure, more true to the inherent qualities of the form, than any other ever written. He has none of the romantic love elements which characterise Shakespeare's comedies and make them so different from Jonson's in subject and mood. He has no one character who looms above the others and with whom we can sympathise. We may admire Face for getting away with more than his fellow-cozeners, but as a knave his mind is never opened to us. His plea in the Epilogue is a further display of his audacity, another of his entertaining tricks. Like all good comedians he keeps us at a distance. He is always a jump ahead, keeping us guessing over what his next trick will be. The chief comedian, perhaps, but firmly a member of the comic ensemble.

As a comedy dealing with man as a social animal it is appropriate that the play's structure should be an intricate web of characters and events. There is never a chance to pause and savour the moment, unless it is over the repellant luxury of Mammon's fantasies. Characters continually come and go. Nobody occupies the centre of the stage for any length of time. Events unroll with a speed and intricacy beyond the power of ordinary humans—even Face—to control. All the disasters—the way the gulls come too thick and fast to be dealt with, the trickery of Surly, the arrival of Lovewit, the treachery of the cozeners to each other—are predicted at some early step in the story and yet not one of them fails to surprise both characters and audience when it happens. Furthermore the interaction of knaves and fools emphasises deceit and illusion. The audience is continually reminded that one character is tricking another, that nobody is honest with anyone else, that most of the gulls are not even honest with themselves. Nothing anybody says can be taken straight. The words in the play belong in a complex of situations and personalities which complicate the surface meaning of every declaration. When Subtle says at I.iv.16 that Mammon has 'talked as [if]he were possessed' about the philosopher's stone, we understand his words on several levels. On the surface it is a simple simile to describe the intensity of Mammon's obsession. Below that we hear the mockery in Subtle's implication that their fish is well hooked. And below that again, the simile, which means that Mammon is behaving as if his body is 'possessed' or inhabited by devils, ought to remind us that Subtle is the Devil in the representation of the three cozeners as the World, the Flesh and the Devil.

Just as he compiled his own theory of comic drama, so Jonson constructed his own plot to exemplify it. He could never have written *The Alchemist* if he had not been a great master of construction. His comic theory demanded both a local subject and a special kind of treatment. The degree of Jonson's originality in this can be seen if you compare his plot with the classical comedy of Plautus (254-184BC), the *Mostellaria,* from which Jonson took his basic situation, a house being put to bad use in its owner's absence. Plautus puts two knaves into the house, the owner's son and his clever servant. Their exploits are chiefly sexual escapades, and the intricate pattern of inversion, the basis of Jonson's moral aim, is lacking together with most of Jonson's power. Jonson acknowledges the *Mostellaria* (V.ii.47 is a direct quotation from it) but he had no real need of it.

Jonson's strength lay in the creative inventiveness which makes not only the plot structure but the poetry, the images of language and structure, so marvellously integral to each other and to Jonson's purpose. The play is a miracle of cohesion in its central idea, in the way the structure embodies that idea, and in the way the poetry upholds the structure.

Poetry

The metaphors of *The Alchemist* pervade its structure and language alike. The patterns of transformation and inversion range from the house itself, transformed from a Blackfriars dwelling-house into a republic of knaves and back again, to the metaphor of Mammon's 'age of gold'. It is an age of gold, but not in the way he wants it to be. The basic metaphor of alchemy is reflected in the structure as each gull is put through the alchemical sequence of ascension, fixation and projection. The whole plot is like the alchemical process, working up, with new ingredients constantly being added, to a grand projection which explodes in everyone's face in the way that the cozeners pretend Subtle's furnace explodes. Everything flies away *'in fumo'* (Subtle's Latin for 'in smoke') in Act V, leaving only shoddy debris, the iron furniture in the cellar.

The alchemical metaphor has implications reaching much further than the plot alone. Subtle the Alchemist is a false creator, a false artist, using his pretended art to make money. He is the antithesis of God the Creator not only as the Devil and as a perverter of words but as a maker of false gods. He makes gold into Mammon's idol. The heat of the alchemical process is like the heat which accompanied the plague, and Subtle as master of the heat of alchemy is the devilish bringer of plague into Lovewit's house. Above all alchemy is the chief metaphor for the false transformations. In the same way that base metals theoretically take their perfect form as gold but in reality stay base, so the cozeners take the outward shape of wise men, kings, generals, the Queen of Faery, but always keep their real shape underneath and in the end return to what they were before they began the alchemical process. Similarly Mammon transforms his proper self, 'a wise sir, at other times', into a fool who puts gold where God should be. The Puritans similarly put Mammon before God, and all the lesser gulls hope to change their natures into something they see (falsely) as better than their basic selves.

In his *Discoveries,* Jonson wrote 'wheresoever manners and fashions are corrupted, language is'. The poetry of *The Alchemist* fully supports this view. Metrically regular throughout, even when a blank verse line is divided across as many as four speakers, its flowing speed and vigour give the play much of its pace and breathlessness. There is never a pause in the regular rhythmical beat of the lines. But the words themselves are corrupted. It is all artificial, in the bad sense of the term. Subtle's poetry is aimed at deceiving others, Mammon's poetry deceives himself. Nowhere are words used honestly. When Dol, pretending to be a studious great lady, says (IV.i.95) 'I am taken, sir,/Whole, with these studies, that contemplate nature', and Mammon replies 'It is a noble humour', we know that she means study of the human body in a sense far removed from what Mammon thinks she means. We applaud Dol, laugh at Mammon, and take note how flexible an instrument language is.

The most obvious way in which language is shown to be corrupted in the play is, of course, in the alchemical cant. In its original forms the language of alchemy was rich in its allusiveness. Fire is a red cockerel, molten iron is the liquor of Mars, the colours produced during the experiments are described as pale citron, the green lion, the peacock's tail or the plumed swan. Exotic names were found for common substances to help them fit the various allegories woven into the mystery of alchemy. Red, the colour which signalled the achievement of the stone, was *sanguis agni,* the blood of the lamb, that is, Christ. The allusiveness of the allegories gave it just enough appearance of meaning to soften the suspicion that it was nothing more than mystifying nonsense. Subtle's use of it emphasises its mystifying qualities and, in the process, discredits it entirely. Subtle's corruption of the serious intentions of the alchemists is one of the transformations which underlines the base metal of the subject when the transformation is reversed. Jonson explodes alchemy as Subtle explodes his own pretence.

Line by line the poetry of the play asserts the patterns of metaphor in which Jonson has placed his realistic characters. There are many smaller patterns arranged around the central metaphor of alchemy.

The pattern of the three cozeners as the World, the Flesh and the Devil has already been noted. Their republic and their separate roles as King, General and Commonwealth likewise can be seen as a pattern of which we are periodically reminded in word or phrase throughout the play. The mercantile language of the cozener's treaty contrasts with the religious language of Mammon's fantasies, both perverted from their proper uses. Military and sexual images also occur to underline the various deceptions. The cozeners are animals, while the gulls are appropriately thought of as birds of various kinds. For Dol the task is 'to pluck his bird as bare as I can' (V.iv.82). Mammon sees himself as a phoenix before he knows himself a gull. Nearly every significant word or phrase spoken in the play fits into one or other of the metaphorical patterns. The play's language is as tightly integrated as its plot structure.

The inversions

It is appropriate to conclude this section about the play as a whole with a word about the patterns of inversion. Inversion is the essential feature of Jonson's kind of comedy. On the model of classical comedy, the initial situation and its development represent a reversed state of normal society. This, in the classical models, might be no more than a temporary disorder, like the *Mostellaria*'s absent house-owner. In *The Alchemist* Jonson inverted everything. Language, reason, truth, law, are all inverted with marvellous consistency.

The proper order of society is replaced by the cozeners' self-sufficient republic, where the only law is their shaky treaty of commercial gain. The same inversion is there in Mammon's New World, in which he believes he will be the sole master. The Puritan brethren similarly want the stone for the unchecked power it will bring them in their new society. Even Dapper, the law clerk, turns a blind eye to the statute forbidding necromancy in his hope of easy money.

The greed which gives Mammon his vision of a new golden world also makes him invert Christian teaching. His God is Mammon, his idol is gold. He sells his character to the Devil (Subtle) for a promise of earthly bliss. All the other gulls, even Surly, reflect in their lesser ways the same inversion of values, personal gain before personal good, the advancement of the material self before the advancement of the spiritual self. The one gull who has enough money to start with, Kastril, ignores his social responsibilities in favour of personal reputation, a shadow. Subtle advises him to sell his land and turn it into gold for the purpose—an echo of Mammon's aim, to turn all his effects into gold, in Kastril's case for a ludicrous ambition which is a parody of Mammon's dream of grandeur.

Greed is the motive common to cozeners and gulls alike. The difference is in their use of language. Truth is universally inverted, by the cozeners deliberately, by the gulls in ignorance and self-deception. The inversion of truth in the play's language is the most pervasive illustration of the upsidedown world which Jonson was concerned to display for the education of his audiences.

The basic metaphor of inversion itself in the play is of course the alchemical transformation. By a process of word-magic and delusion things are made to seem not themselves, and people's natures are transformed by the power of the delusion. In reality nothing changes. Subtle is no king, doctor, magician or alchemist. He is a charlatan. He escapes out of the back door in his natural state. Face resumes his job as Jeremy the servant after an interlude in which he played many roles, none of them his proper self. The transformations were as much an illusion as the idea of alchemical transformation itself. Base metals and base people cannot be turned into gold by easy magic. The only real transformation Jonson hoped for was in the minds of his audience.

Part 4

Hints for study

An outline of a study plan

The chief subjects to study in *The Alchemist* are

- *(i)* how it exemplifies Jonson's theory of comedy
- *(ii)* the structure of the plot
- *(iii)* the central images and plot-metaphors
- *(iv)* the central theme of inversion
- *(v)* the local setting and its relation to realism.

Throughout the play occurrences of the central image-patterns, references to the local London setting, and words such as 'humour' and 'art' which relate to Jonson's theory of comedy need to be noted carefully. The intensity with which Jonson exploits language is one of his chief qualities. Recurrent words and images which should be traced through the play include:

- *(a)* the venture tripartite and the commercial images
- *(b)* the 'republic' or 'common work' of the cozeners and others
- *(c)* the military 'camp' in Lovewit's house
- *(d)* the plague and related allusions to fever, heat and medicine
- *(e)* the alchemical metaphors (ascension, fixation, projection) as they relate to the cozening of the gulls
- *(f)* the animal and bird images applied to the different characters
- *(g)* the images of wealth, spiritual or material
- *(h)* the images of sex, as a marketable commodity.

The realism of the London setting and what that contributes to the play's atmosphere should also be noted. There are references to :

- *(a)* places (Blackfriars, Holborn, the Dagger Inn, Ratcliff, etc.)
- *(b)* people (Dee, Kelley, Read, Ratsey, the players with their Hieronymo costume, etc.)
- *(c)* events (the plague epidemic, the waterworks tax, the Thames freezing over, the lawsuit over Read, etc.)

The plot structures can be studied by drawing up a timetable of the characters' movements on and offstage with the help of the references to the time of day which are made as they come and go. An outline of this timetable has been given in Part 3. A simple linear sketch of who enters and who leaves in each scene (perhaps drawn using different colours to mark the different characters) will help to give a clear picture of how the action develops and how neatly every detail is dovetailed into the main plot structure.

Above all, read the play keeping in mind the situation within which each speech is spoken. When Kastril asks Face if Subtle teaches 'living by the wits' we should appreciate how much more true is Face's assurance that he does than Kastril will ever know. The whole play is built of situations which give the speeches a deeper resonance of implication than the surface meaning provides.

Specimen questions and answers

There are at least four different subject-areas in which questions about *The Alchemist* can usefully be considered. The main ones are:

(i) Jonson's theory of satirical comedy
(ii) the play's realism
(iii) the image-patterns
(iv) the moral force.

Here are four questions, one from each of these subject areas.

(i) How does Jonson's 'humours' idea influence the design of *The Alchemist*?
(ii) In what ways is Jonson's claim to 'show an image of the times' correct?
(iii) How does the imagery of the 'republic' relate to the central themes of the play?
(iv) What sort of justice does the ending of the play exhibit?

Your answers to these questions should take into account all of the following points.

(*i*) How does Jonson's 'humours' idea influence the design of *The Alchemist*?

Jonson believed in the educational and corrective usefulness of art. He thought that the medical theory of a balance of fluids in the body was applicable to the mind as well. A well-balanced mind was a wise mind. Excess of any 'humour' caused folly in the mind in the same way that an imbalance of fluid humours in the body caused physical disease. Just as medicine aimed to correct imbalance in the body, so art should aim to correct mental imbalance. Comedy could do this by displaying mental excesses and holding them up for public ridicule.

In *The Alchemist* Jonson shows the excesses of fools through the behaviour of his gulls. The egomania of Mammon, the 'zeal' of the Puritans, the greed of the lesser gulls and the concern for a reputation, for superficial appearance, in Kastril are the obvious targets for the audience's laughter. In a more complex way the cozeners are also a lesson in excess. Their selfish greed reveals an inverted sense of human and social values. Their commercial treaty, their private republic and, above all, the way they corrupt language from its proper function of telling the truth, show the deeper aspects of mental and moral imbalance. The ease with which they break their treaty and fall back to a position of every man for himself shows how frail and unreliable such an alternative society must be.

The aim of Jonson's art was to educate his audience in the follies and the knaveries which grow from unbalanced humours in human society. *The Alchemist* does so through its intricate web of fools and knaves and the mutually destructive consequences of their self-seeking actions. The temptations of Mammon's Seven Deadly Sins and of the three cozeners as the World, the Flesh and the Devil combine to display how such actions are easy, available, and yet self-defeating.

(ii) In what ways is Jonson's claim to 'show an image of the times' correct?

Jonson's claim in the Prologue of *Every Man in his Humour* to show an image of the times is an echo of Cicero's assertion (see page 12) that art should mirror nature. It is what Hamlet in Shakespeare's play of that name echoes when he tells the players that they in their plays should 'hold the mirror, as 'twere, up to nature'. This however was not for Jonson just a matter of realistically depicting his society. He insisted on the artist's right to make a moral comment on the society he mirrored. The mirror could and should distort, so as to reveal not the surface of society but its essence. And in satire, in stage comedies, that essence should be acknowledged as immoral.

Jonson's rephrasing of Cicero is careful and precise. His art is based on images. He does not simply depict nature realistically but he invents metaphors, notably in *The Alchemist* metaphors of false alchemy and a republic of cozeners, which indicate what he is criticising. His plays mirror the distortions in human society, the ways in which man can distort his proper shape. In the process his images imply what the proper shape ought to be. The realistic details in his mirror are framed in a pattern of metaphors which establish the moral perspective for the whole picture.

In order to have real power and application, Jonson's image is of 'the times', not just of general nature. His targets are here and now, in his contemporary audience. The evidence to prove the truth of his assertions about man's distortion of his proper image is present for everyone to see. Therefore his satirical comedies are packed with local details and references to everyday things and people known to all his audience. People in 'the times' of his day think of 'manners', moral behaviour, as mere 'humours'. The artist's duty is to point out such foolishness for what it is.

Jonson's 'realism' is, therefore, of a special kind. He is not primarily concerned to convince us that we might find Subtles and Mammons in the street around us. As Musgrove says in the introduction to his edition of *The Alchemist*, 'nobody on earth ever behaved like these creatures' (page 2). They are exaggerations, caricatures designed to emphasise the dangerous tendencies in Jonson's society, not figures in a normal mirror of reality. Jonson's realism is different from the realism of nineteenth and twentieth-century fiction, drama and cinema because his aim was different. Merely holding a mirror up for people to see themselves he would have thought pointless. His plays are images not of normality but of what he saw as abnormality.

(*iii*) How does the imagery of the 'republic' relate to the central themes of the play?

All the specific images in *The Alchemist* are interrelated. Each group of images has its bearing on the central theme of the play, and has parallels with the other central images. The image of Lovewit's house as a republic or free state is a good illustration of this. It is an inversion or parody of a proper state of society, with Subtle as its king or sovereign, Face as its general and chief defender, and Dol as the 'commonwealth', or property they share. The house is a military camp fortified against the outside world. Its laws are the indenture tripartite, the commercial treaty or 'venture' whereby the members of the republic agree to cooperate for their mutual commercial benefit. Like all the other inversions, this is not a real creation. It is a temporary transformation as false as the alchemical transformation of base metal into gold. Even before the outside world applies any pressure on it, the treaty has begun to break under the weight of Subtle's and Face's greed for Dame Pliant. In the end it breaks, and leaves little evidence that it ever existed, like the remains of the alchemical projection.

There are several parallels in the play to this inverted society of the cozeners. Mammon's new world, his new age of gold, and the 'separated' society of the Puritan brethren both deny ordinary social laws in favour of a self-seeking republic of their own. Dapper too denies the validity of the law in his own interest. And in Act V Lovewit inverts the proper society of his own household by agreeing to be ruled by his servant.

In the action of the play the republic is an area requiring defence. Visually the action centres on the main door which gives access from the outside world to the cozeners' republic and vice versa. The plague imagery represents the cozeners as an epidemic infesting the house in contrast with the outside world which has been freed from sickness. Gulls from the world outside are infected with the republic's sickness, which is greed, and suffer accordingly. Only outside the house can Mammon and the others learn the truth about the cozening. Not of course that the outside world is healthy. All the scenes set in the street outside the door are marked by disagreements. Mammon argues with Surly. The Puritans argue with each other. Face argues with the neighbours when Lovewit arrives. Nobody outside the door knows what is going on inside. Even at the end, with the republic broken, the plague cleared away and order restored, Lovewit only stands as master by virtue of a new treaty with his servant. Nothing has really been transformed.

(iv) What sort of justice does the ending of the play exhibit?

Lovewit and Face seem to get off in the conclusion with more than anyone else. Mammon and the other gulls lose a lot of their money and property. Surly fails to capture the rich widow. Subtle and Dol escape no better off than before they met Face. Face is back as Jeremy the butler, but he has Lovewit's promise to 'help his fortune' (V.v.151), and he is the only character in the whole play not to be gulled at some point or other. He gulls Subtle and Dol out of their loot, and gulls Lovewit into taking him back as butler in a new alliance. Nobody defeats Face. Lovewit of course ends up with all the material wealth, the trunks full of the cozeners' loot, the brass, pewter and ironware in the cellar, and the rich widow as his wife. Inevitably audiences and critics have asked why Lovewit should triumph in this way when he has done nothing to deserve it.

Some views focus on Lovewit as the exemplification of the spirit of comedy. His is the lover of wit, a lord of misrule who presides over a disorderly world for the fun it brings. In his edition Musgrove concludes that Lovewit completes the circle of gulling: 'the transformations leave men as they were; but the laughter that follows them into the streets of Blackfriars has a quality of ease' (p. 6). Other critics have seen Jonson as in effect shrugging his shoulders and saying that this is the way things are. Jackson (pp. 68-9), Kernan (p. 85) and Dessen (p. 137) all consider that in the ending of *The Alchemist* Jonson relaxes the stern moral view evident in, for instance, *Volpone*.

All such views miss the point that Jonson's main concern was not with the fate of his characters but with the fate of his audience. The characters are fictions, his audiences are real. If Lovewit and Face get off lightly that may be the way things are in life, but it is not therefore a matter to approve of morally.

In the play foolishness makes its own punishment, and quick wit makes its own reward. Greed brings no reward either to fool or knave. Only a cheerful adaptability and good humour—or good 'humour'— towards whatever fortune may provide can bring reward. Neither fate, good or bad, matters as much as the recognition of what values are inverted and what the consequences of the inversion can be.

The consequences are good for Lovewit, moderate for Face (or rather Jeremy) and bad for the others. In no case do we see justice being done. There is no legal justice to punish the crimes of the cozeners. There is no poetic justice to clinch the humiliation of all the gulls. Dapper and Drugger never even learn that they have been gulled. Lovewit is gulled by Face and cheerfully enjoys the rewards it brings him. There is a kind of justice in Mammon choosing to lose the wealth he has poured into Lovewit's house rather than admit in public that he has been gulled. His greed has been made to learn its limits. There is a kind of ironic justice, too, when Surly, so clever at seeing through the alchemical pretence and at disguising himself as a Spaniard, fails in the end to see through Face's disguise as Jeremy, or rather that Face was the disguise and Jeremy the reality. But these are minor ironic details. There is no grand conclusion of poetic justice.

Part 5

Suggestions for further reading

The text

The Alchemist is best studied in an edition with detailed explanatory notes. Currently available texts containing *The Alchemist* on its own include S. Musgrove's edition in the Fountainwell Drama Texts series, published by Oliver and Boyd, Edinburgh, 1968, and Douglas Brown's New Mermaid text published by Benn, London, 1966. Musgrove's has the better notes, and the text is in Jonson's own spelling. This helps to clarify some of his puns and wordplay, but may give some difficulty to the reader who is not familiar with Elizabethan English and its variations from modern English. The glossary at the back of the Musgrove edition is helpful with this kind of problem, however. The edition with most notes (provided helpfully at the foot of the page) is that of F. H. Mares in the Revels series, Methuen, London, 1967. Alvin Kernan has also edited the play in *The Yale Ben Jonson*, Yale University Press, New Haven, 1974.

Other works by Jonson

Of Jonson's other plays *Volpone* (1605) is probably the most rewarding, and the one usually ranked with *The Alchemist* as his best work. *Bartholomew Fair* (1614) has qualities similar to those of *The Alchemist* in many ways, though it lacks the cohesion of plot structure and the tight link between the language and the central images of the play. It deals with London life in ways which add something to the portrayal of London characters in *The Alchemist*.

Students who wish to look more closely at Jonson's theories of art should look at *Timber: or Discoveries*. This is a loose collection of jottings together with more considered passages which were found after his death and published in 1640. They are not highly organised, and can be skimmed through for the most part. The most polished section deals with literary criticism. What he writes there about language has a particular significance for *The Alchemist,* in the respect he shows for its proper use and in his regard for plain speaking even amongst the most learned writers. *Discoveries* is printed in the Herford and Simpson collected edition of Jonson's *Works,* Clarendon

Press, Oxford, 1925-52, Vol. VIII. Parts of it are also available in various collections of criticism, for instance *English Critical Essays XVI-XVIII Centuries,* ed. Edmund D. Jones, Oxford University Press in the World Classics series.

General Reading

Background

Amongst the critical works which deal helpfully with various aspects of the background to *The Alchemist* are:

BOUGHNER, J. C.: *The Devil's Disciple: Ben Jonson's Debt to Machiavelli,* Philosophical Library, New York, 1968.

BRADBROOK, M. C.: *The Growth and Structure of Elizabethan Comedy,* Chatto, London, 1955.

GIBBONS, BRIAN: *Jacobean City Comedy,* Hart-Davis, London, 1968.

GURR, ANDREW: *The Shakespearean Stage 1574-1642,* Cambridge University Press, Cambridge, 1970.

KERNAN, ALVIN: *The Cankered Muse,* Yale University Press, New Haven, Connecticut, 1959.

KNIGHTS, L. C.: *Drama and Society in the Age of Jonson,* Chatto, London, 1937.

PARFITT, GEORGE: *Ben Jonson: Public Poet and Private Man,* Dent, London, 1976.

Criticism

The major critical books which have the most valuable things to say about *The Alchemist* are

BARISH, JONAS A.: *Ben Jonson and the Language of Prose Comedy,* Harvard University Press, Cambridge (Mass.), 1960.

BARTON, ANNE: *Ben Jonson, Dramatist*, Cambridge University Press, Cambridge, 1984.

DESSEN, ALAN C.: *Jonson's Moral Comedy,* Northwestern University Press, Chicago, 1971.

JACKSON, G. B.: *Vision and Judgement in Ben Jonson's Drama,* Yale University Press, New Haven, 1968.

PARTRIDGE, E. B.: *The Broken Compass,* Chatto, London, 1958.

THAYER, C. G.: *Ben Jonson. Studies in the Plays,* University of Oklahoma Press, Norman, 1963.

There is also a useful book of essays by different authors on various aspects of Jonson's work: *Ben Jonson: a Collection of Critical Essays,* ed. Jonas A. Barish, Prentice-Hall, Englewood Cliffs, New Jersey, 1963. This includes an essay by Paul Goodman, 'Comic Plots: *The Alchemist*'.

Other articles with useful material relevant to the play include:

ARMSTRONG, WILLIAM A.: 'Ben Jonson and Jacobean Stagecraft', in *Jacobean Theatre,* eds. J. R. Brown and Bernard Harris, Edward Arnold, London, 1960.

DUNCAN, E. H.: 'Jonson's *The Alchemist* and the Literature of Alchemy', *PMLA* LXI (1946), pp.699-710.

REDWINE, J. D.: 'Beyond Psychology.' The Moral Basis of Jonson's Theory of Humour Characterisation', *E.L.H.* XXVIII (1961), pp.316-34.

The author of these notes

ANDREW GURR, who is Professor of English at the University of Reading, was previously a senior lecturer at the University of Leeds, Professor at the University of Nairobi, Kenya, and visiting Lecturer at the University. of Auckland. He was educated at the University of Auckland (New Zealand) and is Ph.D. of the University of Cambridge, where he also taught for several years. His publications include *The Shakespearean Stage 1574-1642,* (1970), *Hamlet and the Distracted Globe* (1979), and editions of plays by Beaumont and Fletcher. He has also written on Shakespeare, as well as on the literature of Africa and New Zealand. He is currently editor of the *Journal of Commonwealth Literature.*

York Notes: list of titles

Choice of Poets
Nineteenth Century Short Stories
Poetry of the First World War
Six Women Poets

CHINUA ACHEBE
Things Fall Apart

EDWARD ALBEE
Who's Afraid of Virginia Woolf?

MAYA ANGELOUS
I know Why the Caged Bird Sings

MARGARET ATWOOD
Cat's Eye
The Handmaid's Tale

JANE AUSTEN
Emma
Mansfield Park
Northanger Abbey
Persuasion
Pride and Prejudice
Sense and Sensibility

SAMUEL BECKETT
Waiting for Godot

ALAN BENNETT
Talking Heads

JOHN BETJEMAN
Selected Poems

WILLIAM BLAKE
Songs of Innocence, Songs of Experience

ROBERT BOLT
A Man For All Seasons

HAROLD BRIGHOUSE
Hobson's Choice

CHARLOTTE BRONTË
Jane Eyre

EMILY BRONTË
Wuthering Heights

ROBERT BURNS
Selected Poems

BYRON
Selected Poems

GEOFFREY CHAUCER
The Franklin's Tale
The Merchant's Tale
The Miller's Tale
The Nun's Priest's Tale
Prologue to the Canterbury Tales
The Wife of Bath's Tale

SAMUEL TAYLOR COLERIDGE
Selected Poems

JOSEPH CONRAD
Heart of Darkness

DANIEL DEFOE
Moll Flanders
Robinson Crusoe

SHELAGH DELANEY
A Taste of Honey

CHARLES DICKENS
Bleak House
David Copperfield
Great Expectations
Hard Times
Oliver Twist

EMILY DICKINSON
Selected Poems

JOHN DONNE
Selected Poems

DOUGLAS DUNN
Selected Poems

GEORGE ELIOT
Middlemarch
The Mill on the Floss
Silas Marner

T. S. ELIOT
Selected Poems
The Waste Land

HENRY FIELDING
Joseph Andrews

F. SCOTT FITZGERALD
The Great Gatsby

E. M. FORSTER
Howards End
A Passage to India

JOHN FOWLES
The French Lieutenant's Woman

BRIAN FRIEL
Translations

ELIZABETH GASKELL
North and South

WILLIAM GOLDING
Lord of the Flies

OLIVER GOLDSMITH
She Stoops to Conquer

GRAHAM GREENE
Brighton Rock

WILLIS HALL
The Long, The Short and The Tall

THOMAS HARDY
Far from the Madding Crowd
Jude the Obscure
The Mayor of Casterbridge
Selected Poems
Tess of the D'Urbervilles

L. P. HARTLEY
The Go-Between

NATHANIEL HAWTHORNE
The Scarlet Letter

SEAMUS HEANEY
Selected Poems

ERNEST HEMINGWAY
The Old Man and the Sea

SUSAN HILL
I'm the King of the Castle

BARRY HINES
A Kestrel for a Knave

HOMER
The Iliad
The Odyssey

ALDOUS HUXLEY
Brave New World

BEN JONSON
The Alchemist
Volpone

JAMES JOYCE
Dubliners
A Portrait of the Artist as a Young Man

JOHN KEATS
Selected Poems

PHILIP LARKIN
Selected Poems

D. H. LAWRENCE
The Rainbow
Sons and Lovers
Women in Love

LOUISE LAWRENCE
Children of the Dust

HARPER LEE
To Kill a Mockingbird

LAURIE LEE
Cider with Rosie

CHRISTOPHER MARLOWE
Doctor Faustus

ARTHUR MILLER
The Crucible
Death of a Salesman
A View from the Bridge

JOHN MILTON
Paradise Lost I & II
Paradise Lost IV & IX

TONI MORRISON
Beloved

SEAN O'CASEY
Juno and the Paycock

GEORGE ORWELL
Animal Farm
Nineteen Eighty-four

JOHN OSBORNE
Look Back in Anger

WILFRED OWEN
Selected Poems

HAROLD PINTER
The Caretaker

SYLVIA PLATH
Selected Works

ALEXANDER POPE
Selected Poems

J. B. PRIESTLEY
An Inspector Calls

JEAN RHYS
The Wide Sargasso Sea

WILLY RUSSELL
Educating Rita
Our Day Out

J. D. SALINGER
The Catcher in the Rye

WILLIAM SHAKESPEARE
Antony and Cleopatra
As You Like It
Coriolanus
Hamlet
Henry IV Part I
Henry V
Julius Caesar
King Lear
Macbeth
Measure for Measure
The Merchant of Venice
A Midsummer Night's Dream
Much Ado About Nothing
Othello
Richard II
Richard III
Romeo and Juliet
Sonnets
The Taming of the Shrew
The Tempest
Twelfth Night
The Winter's Tale

GEORGE BERNARD SHAW
Arms and the Man
Pygmalion
Saint Joan

MARY SHELLEY
Frankenstein

RICHARD BRINSLEY SHERIDAN
The Rivals

R. C. SHERRIFF
Journey's End

RUKSHANA SMITH
Salt on the Snow

MURIEL SPARK
The Prime of Miss Jean Brodie

JOHN STEINBECK
The Grapes of Wrath
Of Mice and Men
The Pearl

TOM STOPPARD
Rosencrantz and Guildenstern are Dead

ROBERT LOUIS STEVENSON
Dr Jekyll and Mr Hyde

JONATHAN SWIFT
Gulliver's Travels

ROBERT SWINDELLS
Daz for Zoe

JOHN MILLINGTON SYNGE
The Playboy of the Western World

MILDRED D. TAYLOR
Roll of Thunder, Hear My Cry

W. M. THACKERAY
Vanity Fair

MARK TWAIN
Huckleberry Finn

VIRGIL
The Aeneid

DEREK WALCOTT
Selected Poems

ALICE WALKER
The Color Purple

JAMES WATSON
Talking in Whispers

JOHN WEBSTER
The Duchess of Malfi

OSCAR WILDE
The Importance of Being Earnest

TENNESSEE WILLIAMS
Cat on a Hot Tin Roof
A Streetcar Named Desire

VIRGINIA WOOLF
Mrs Dalloway
To the Lighthouse

WILLIAM WORDSWORTH
Selected Poems

W. B. YEATS
Selected Poems